DISTANCE EDUCATION AND STUDENT SUPPORT SERVICES

DISTANCE EDUCATION AND STUDENT SUPPORT SERVICES

Prof. Dhaneswar Harichandan
Director
Institute of Distance Education
University of Mumbai, Vidyanagari
Santacruz (E), Mumbai (Maharashtra)

DEEP & DEEP PUBLICATIONS PVT. LTD.
F-159, Rajouri Garden, New Delhi - 110 027

DISTANCE EDUCATION AND STUDENT SUPPORT SERVICES

ISBN 978-81-8450-184-1

Printed in India at MAYUR ENTERPRISES
WZ Plot No. 3, Gujjar Market, Tihar Village, New Delhi - 110 018

Published by DEEP & DEEP PUBLICATIONS PVT. LTD.,
F-159, Rajouri Garden, New Delhi - 110 027 • Phone : 25435369, 25440916
E-mail : ddpubs@gmail.com • ddpbooks@yahoo.co.in
Showroom :
2/13, Ansari Road, Daryaganj, New Delhi - 110 002 • Telefax : 23245122

Contents

Acknowledgements

The origin of this research dates back to 1991 when I was awarded ICSSR Doctoral Fellowship at Indian Institute of Education, Pune under the guidance of Dr. P.R. Panchamukhi. It could not be materialized until I was introduced to Dr. Sridhar B. Gogate who readily accepted to guide me under YCMOU. I am really indebted to him for his encouragement, love and sympathy shown to me without which this work would not have been completed. In a way this work is the culmination of ten years of toiling in this field.

I wish to thank the distance learners who had taken time in filling up the lengthy questionnaire. Thanks are due to the Director of the IDE, University of Mumbai and Coordinator IGNOU study centre. It is my hope that the findings of the research will strengthen the endeavours of dual mode universities in implementing the good practices of Support Services.

I express my thanks to Dr. Vasudha Kamat, CIET, New Delhi who always inspired me to complete my Ph.D., Dr. Shrawan Kejariwal, JNU, who introduced me to my guide, Dr. Anant Joshi, YCMOU for the academic support, and of course my wife Swarna and son Mickey for the patience and encouragement.

Finally, while I acknowledge the above persons, the shortcomings remain are mine only.

Dhaneswar Harichandan

Abbreviations

IDE	:	Institute of Distance Education
IGNOU	:	Indira Gandhi National Open University
UKOU	:	United Kingdom Open University
EADTU	:	European Association of Distance Teaching Universities
PCP	:	Personal Contact Programme
SC	:	Study Centre
ARS	:	Assignment Response Sheet
SM	:	Study Material
SIM	:	Self Instructional Material
SSS	:	Student Support Services
OU	:	Open University
DEI	:	Distance Education Institute
DEC	:	Distance Education Council
UGC	:	University Grants Commission

1

Distance Education : Concept and Growth

1.1 INTRODUCTION

"It is the development of distance education as an academic discipline that will have the most profound effect on its practice in the future". (Gough, 1984). Since then distance education has grown world-wide. In the 1980's distance education emerged as a standard component of the provision of education in many countries. In contrast with conventional education which is oral and group-based, distance education shatters the interpersonal communication of face to face provision and disperses the learning group throughout the nation.

For long the cinderella of the education spectrum, distance education emerged in the 1970's with a changed image. It has recently come of age after a chequered and often criticized first one hundred years. Furthermore, its future seems assured because of the growing privatisation of life and the incapacity of conventional education system to cope with even minimal educational opportunity elsewhere.

1.1.1. Correspondence Education

Distance education is a generic term that includes the range of teaching/learning strategies referred to as :

Correspondence Education
External study
Extra Mural system
Home Study
Independent Study
Off Campus Programme
Out reach
Open learning
Open education

Correspondence education is defined in the UNESCO volume Terminology of Adult Education as : Education conducted by the postal services without face to face contact between teacher and learner. Teaching is done by written or tape recorded materials sent to the learner whose progress is monitored through written or taped exercises to the teacher, who corrects them and returns to the learner with criticisms and advice (UNESCO, 1979).

The main problem with the term correspondence education is that it cannot encompass the didactic potential of this form of education in the 1980's. Critics of the term tend to associate correspondence education with some of the less successful aspects of distance education in the past and to feel that this term contributes to the still questioned status of study at a distance.

1.1.2 Distance Education

Distance education is a suitable term to bring together both the teaching and learning elements of this field of education. Distance teaching indicates the process of course development by which a distance institution prepares learning materials for students, emphasizing on the role of teacher, while distance learning is a process as seen from the students perspective. The relationship of distance teaching and distance learning may be shown thus :

FIG. 1.1

Relationship of Distance Teaching to Distance Education

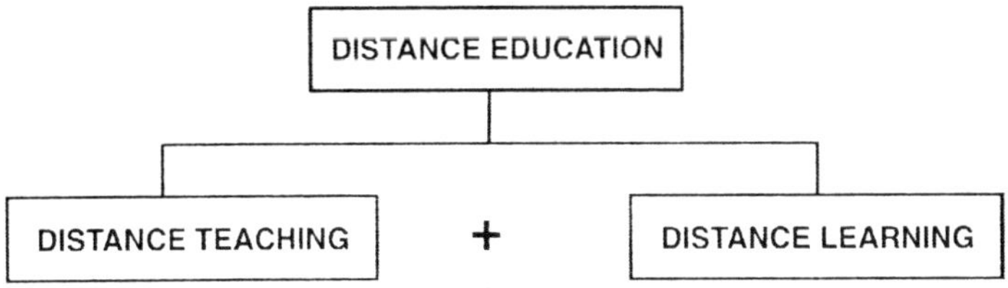

The term distance education has gained in strength and acceptance. It indicates well the basic characteristics of this form of education, the separation of teacher and learner which distinguishes it from conventional oral, group-based education. It also encompasses well the two characteristic operating systems unique to the distance education, the *course development sub-system* (distance teaching) and a *student support sub-system* (distance learning).

At its 12th world conference in 1982 at Vancouver, British Columbia, the International Council for Correspondence Education debated the question of nomenclature for the form of education under discussion. The Council decided to change its name to the International Council for Distance Education, thus giving international sanction to the use of the term distance education. An international council does not change its name lightly and when it does, it accepts that the advantages of the change counter-balance the claims of the previous title.

1.1.3 Open Education

In the 1990's the International Council for Distance Education has been re-christened as International Council for Open and Distance Education giving further impetus to the term open education.

There is extensive overlap between the use of the term "Open Education" and "Distance Education". The decision of the United Kingdom Government in the Mid-1960's to rename the "University of the Air" to the "Open University" popularised the term "Open". It is found in the titles of the distance teaching universities in India, Pakistan, Srilanka, Thailand and Venezuela.

Escotet (1980) distinguishes the terms as :

> Open Education is particularly characterised by the removal of restrictions, exclusions and privileges; by the accreditation of student's previous experiences, by the flexibility of the management of the time variable, and by substantial changes in the traditional relationship between professors and students. On the other hand, distance education is a modality which permits the delivery of a group of didactic media without the necessity of regular class participation, where the individual is responsible for his own learning.

1.2 GROWTH OF DISTANCE EDUCATION INSTITUTES

Distance Education Institutes and open university have now become an international phenomenon. Increasing social acceptance also makes it a vital component of higher education. The Indian distance higher education today comprises 14 open universities, 125 university Distance Education Institutes/Correspondence Course Institutes, and many private or autonomous providers in government and non-government sectors. Now, about two million students studying through this mode constitute nearly 20 percent of the total enrolment in higher education in the country. All the open universities put together are enrolling 616 thousand students each year and these numbers are bound to grow in future. In 2001 they offered 294 educational training and extension programmes comprising 1960 courses, offered with the help of 98 regional centres, 3137 study centres, 38,662 counsellors, and 3449 full time staff. Nearly 203 thousand students (excluding certificates and diplomas) have graduated for degree programmes. While the state open universities serve the educational and training needs of their respective states, IGNOU has international jurisdiction (Dikshit, 2002).

TABLE 1.1
Growth of Enrolment in Distance Education

Year	Enrolment in Higher education	Enrolment in Distance education	Total Enrolment in Higher Education (ii + iii)	Share of Distance education (iii) as % of (iv)
(i)	(ii)	(iii)	(iv)	(v)
1975-76	24.9	0.6	25.5	2.3
1981-82	31.5	1.9	33.4	5.7
1990-91	49.9	5.6	55.5	10.1
1999-2000	77.3	15.8	93.1	17.0

Source : Basic Statistics relating to Distance Education Institutions in India, DEC-IGNOU, New Delhi, 2001.

TABLE 1.2
Enrolment in Distance Education Institutes by Region 2000

Distance Education Institutions	Region				Total
	North	South	East	West	
(a) Open Universitites (Number)	3	2	2	3	10
(b) Total Enrolment	2,97,435	1,39,406	4019	1,77,435	6,16,295
(c) (% of the Total)	(48.26)	(22.62)	(0.65)	(23.79)	(100.00)
(a) Correspondence course Institutes (Number)	15	25	11	13	64
(b) Total Enrolment	2,61,555	6,04,502	41,250	54,673	9,63,980
(c) (% of the Total)	(27.13)	(62.70)	(4.27)	(5.67)	(100.00)
Total enrolment (% of the Total)	5,58,990 (33.37)	7,43,908 (47.07)	45,269 (2.87)	2,32,108 (14.68)	15,80,275 (100.00)

Source: Basic Statistics relating to Distance Education Institutions in India, DEC-IGNOU, New Delhi, 2001.

TABLE 1.3
Number of Countries and Distance Education Institutes by Region 2000

Regions	*Number of Countries*	*Number of Institutes*
Africa	34	122
Asia	18	97
Australia	4	66
Middle East	2	3
Europe	18	207
North America	2	217
Caribbean	4	7
Latin America	13	60
	95	779

Source : Kumar, 1998.

1.3 STUDENT SUPPORT SERVICES

All activities involved in facilitating the learning process of Distance Education Institutes are termed as student support services. Student support services cover a wide range of functions, starting from producing the learning materials and making them available to students upto arranging contact programmes and conducting examinations (Koul & Ramanujam, 1989). In distance mode of education there is a dire need of support services because students are separated from teachers and the learner groups are heterogenous and spread across the country. Williams and Williams (1987) emphasised that increasingly Distance Education Institutes are acknowledging that their students need support beyond what is provided by teaching staff and study materials. Infact the development and continuous improvement of support services is a vital aspect of distance education system. The support service bridges the gap of isolation and injects the touch of teacherhood to the distance learner. In specific terms, it helps in counselling, continuous assessment and facilitates the learning process.

The provision of Student Support Services achieves for distance education systems, the essential feed-back mechanism that are characteristics of education. It is mainly through them that two-way communication is established between student and institute. Provision of Student Support Services distinguishes Distance Education Institutes. from publishing houses and other producers of learning materials.

Most of the support services of all Distance Education Institutes of the world are provided in the form of standard course package, like print materials accompanied by self-assessment and revision exercises, laboratory kit etc. The complimentary course material is given in the form of video and audio cassettes. The inter-activity is provided through correspondence, computer tele and video conferencing, etc. Counselling is carried out in the form of face to face interaction and through other electronic media. In all cases, study centres play a very vital role in providing support services to distance learners.

The following paragraphs details the provision of Student Support Services in the universities of the present study.

1.3.1 Support Services in IGNOU

Existing Support Services

Indira Gandhi National Open University is an apex body to impart distance education across the country. The university has established a strong student support service. It provides support services through the head office, 62 regional centers and 2053 study centers spread all over the country, 17 recognized regional centers catering to Army, Airforce and Navy personnel. These centers operate under single window system. The headquarter decides the policies and the modalities of student support services and the major work is carried out by the study centers. Regional centres play an intermediary link between study centers and the headquarters. In IGNOU, about 21,000 part-time counsellors are engaged in counselling the distant learners. To respond to the problems of its learners, IGNOU has established a *student welfare cell* located in the vice-chancellor's office. The student services center at the headquarters and regional centers report to the cell. As far as quality assurance is concerned, IGNOU has established Distance Education Council (DEC) for coordination and maintenance of standards in distance and open education system in the country.

The delivery mechanism plays a vital role in the distance education system because learning materials are to be made easily accessible to the distant learners. In order to ensure accessibility the major units of support services, i.e. Regional Centres, Study Centres and Electronic Media Production Centre require to adopt an effective delivery mechanism. According to Prof. Gandhi (1994) the other crucial areas that need to be strengthened are the support services through the network of Regional Centres, Study Centres and the Communication Division. In order to provide flexibility and suitability of a large number of distant learners the University plans to adopt different varieties of Study Centres. These include :

Study centres
Recognised study centres
Sub-study centres
Programme study centres
Work centres
Satellite learning centres
Mobile study centres

In areas where study centers are not available the innovative concept of the distance learning facilitators (DLF) has been put in place. A DLF is an effective mechanism to utilise educated and trained human resources to provide support to students.

Electronic media has become very prominent in the distant mode of education. IGNOU has also caught the race of communication revolution and started the Teleconferencing system in the country. The system being interactive, has an immense potential to facilitate the learning process. The University is planning to establish 135 receive sites. The immense potential of the electronic media has evoked the thinking of distant educationists to exploit the media

1.3.2 Support Services in IDE

The Institute of Distance Education of University of

Mumbai follows the multimedia approach in the teaching learning process. It comprises of :

- Printed study materials in English (Marathi also for under graduate courses in selected subjects only).
- Supporting Audio-Video programmes.
- Face to Face interaction with teachers at personal contact programme centres in the constituent colleges and also at headquarters.
- Counselling at headquarters by the core faculty.
- Library and reading hall facilities including home lending of books.
- Assignments for assessment and feed-back on the response sheets (MA Education, PGDFM & PGDORM course only).

The institute is now having a Virtual Learning Centre from where live lectures can be transmitted and received through edusat and there in two way audio and video interaction with the students and the faculty.

2

Studies on Distance Education

2.1 INTRODUCTION

Student support service is an important aspect of distance education system. Being an innovative system it has always been open to all-teaching methods and media. It combines both teaching and learning activities. Various communication technology devices have been integrated in to this system. These have come to be recognized as an effective support service both for the teacher and the learner. The developing countries need to be careful in developing media support which is relevant to their conditions. Considering the significance of this area in the field of distance education, as in any other field, some literature in the form of conceptual framework, or model and theoretical aspects explaining the support service is available. Besides this, some studies have been conducted in India and abroad dealing with the student support service. This chapter deals with the need and importance of review of related literature followed by a brief review of the theoretical papers, articles, research reports, dissertations, etc. It may be mentioned that only those portions of the literature reviewed are presented here which have relevance to this study.

2.2 NEED AND IMPORTANCE OF REVIEW OF RELATED LITERATURE

A review of previous literature on the topic is an essential component of research. It demonstrates an understanding of the existing literature pertinent to the study and investigation. "Review" according to Webster's Dictionary (1987) is to "examine again, study critically, general survey, critique". In research, review of related literature means to conduct general survey of related studies to analyze them critically and put them logically such that a certain framework and dimension can emerge. Based on this a researcher can look for missing links in the chain of knowledge continuum. These can be considered to be the 'gaps' or needs and a researcher can initiate work on these gaps. Thus, review of related literature throws light on the studies available and enables the researcher to finalise the topic of the study.

Review of a good number of area-based studies can prove to be very helpful in enabling a researcher to understand how researchers in different parts of the world have studied various issues. It also avoids possible duplications where it is not called for. Some of the answers to the questions may also be obtained from the researches that have already been conducted. It is not true that review of studies is required only at the initial phase of research initiation, but is also required to support a researcher in identification of objectives and formulation of research questions and hypothesis. Review is useful in supporting and justifying the need for a study. Further, the reviewed studies are also of great help when the researcher completes the analysis part of the research, where one needs to compare the results in the light of the other study findings. Hence, the review is more or less a continuous activity.

A review of related literature is both essential and useful for mapping the research landscape in the relevant area of research so that one becomes acquainted with the present status of research and aware of the grey areas where work is either non-existent or sparse. In this chapter an attempt is made to project the research literature available in the country and abroad on Student Support Services.

2.3 DEVELOPMENT OF DISTANCE EDUCATION RESEARCH

Research on distance education is a post-World War II development, and published research monographs are a phenomenon of 1960's (Holmberg, 1987). In 1960, the first monograph (Holmberg, 1960) and the first bibliography (Child's, 1960) of distance education appeared. Holmberg notes that like most educational research studies on distance education were from the beginning based both on intellectual inquisitiveness generally and also on practical requirements implying, among other things, a desire to know as a result of feelings of social and educational responsibility among practitioners. During the 1970's and 1980's when distance education research seems to have come of age, it is from the distance teaching organisation that most research studies emanate (Holmberg, 1990).

Important reviews and debates on distance education research in recent times include the following : Morgan (1984), Minnis (1985), Holmberg (1989), Marland (1989), Cookson (1989), Panda (1992), Sahoo (1991). On the status of contemporary research on distance education, Moore (1985) made certain important observations "the general conclusion I was left with from this review of the past twenty years is that the condition of research in distance education is about what might be expected at this early stage in the growth of a new field of education . . . Considering the expansion of the field, there now being hundreds of thousands more students and hundreds of new institutions with investments of millions of dollars and considering the existence of several international journals and professional associations and the great volume of words now written about distance education, one must conclude that the volume of good research has not kept pace with this growth". Commenting on the earlier studies, he further notes: "It is the proportion of well designed research, research which is generalizable beyond the immediate population or events under study which has declined".

2.4 OVERVIEW OF DISTANCE EDUCATION LITERATURE IN INDIA

Despite distance education has been in vogue in the form of correspondence education right since 1962, as a major area of academic study and debate, this is comparative a recent development. Planning and management of distance education as a major area of study and training was initiated by National Institute of Educational Planning and Administration (NIEPA) which regularly brought together all the directors of distance education from various universities (Mukhopadhyay, 1990). Subsequently, NIEPA also promoted a series of research studies on the planning and management of distance education. Before such organised effort of NIEPA, research on distance education was almost single handedly contributed by Prof. Ruddar Datt and a few other scholars for doctoral studies. Before this visible movement, distance education institutes clubbed themselves under the auspices of Indian Council of Distance Education for several years. The Indian literature on distance education is largely the outcome of the seminars in which ICDE conferences and/or anthologies by various scholars with a few exceptions of authored volumes on the subject Doctoral studies in distance education though fifteen in number are very few when compared to 3785 such studies in education completed by the end of 1990 (Buch, 1991). Since very few studies have been conducted in the areas of distance education in India, we will first discuss in brief researches on distance education in its entirety to be followed by researches conducted on student support service which is our main concern. Since distance education is a reality in India, studies classified under correspondence education and open universities are taken under one umbrella.

2.5 RESEARCH STUDIES IN INDIA

The first research study (M.Ed. dissertation) on correspondence education was undertaken in 1972 (Sashi, 1972). It related to the achievement of regular and correspondence students. A study was conducted on the trend enrolment in correspondence courses from 1971 to 1976 taking into consideration the nature of courses, annual compound rate of enrolment and levels of courses (Datt, 1976). Other studies conducted in the areas of growth of the system of distance education highlight the gradual growth of distance education in the country which are usually a mere extension of the system of the regular courses offered through universities, Anand (1979) Biswal (1979), Khan (1982), Datt (1984), Sahoo (1985), Balasubramanian (1986).

The studies conducted on different aspects of Student Support Services are as follows :

1. *Print-based study material*: This has been witnessed that all of the DEI as well as OU give emphasis on print-based instructional materials. The materials may be modular forms of SIM and some other types as per certain formats as prescribed by respective institutes (Biswal, 1979, Singh, 1980, Khan, 1982, Singh, 1983, Sahoo, 1985). These studies addresses as the issues pertaining to usefulness of print materials, difficulties of students in reading the study materials, etc.
2. *Assignments* : Assignment system is treated as one of the key components of Student Support Service in Distance Education. Assignment was found most useful by the students of Universities like H.P. University (Biswal, 1979) and Regional Colleges of Education (Kumar, 1986). Most of the students appreciated compulsory submission of assignments since most of the students received evaluated response sheets in time (Sahoo, 1985). Distance Education institutions did not make serious efforts to clarify students doubts (Dewal, 1982, Nagaraj, 1982, Sahoo, 1985).
3. *Personal Contact Programme* : All the institutions of Distance Education had the provision of PCP (Datt, 1976 and Biswal, 1979). Compulsion, optional provision of attendance, selection of venue of PCP, lack of proper facilities, acted as influential factors in students attendance in PCP (Sahoo, 1985).
4. *Study Centre* : Working of the study centres : A case of two open universities, this project was submitted to

SNDTW University. This highlights that the facilities at the study centres are grossly underutilised (Harichandan, 1990). Other related studies are conducted by Chandhok (1995), Mani (1989), Srinivasa Charyulu (1992), Devi, Usha (1994) and Vijaya (1993).

2.6 RESEARCH STUDIES ABROAD

Although substantial literature on methodologies relating to the production of learning materials and resources for Open and Distance Education are available, relatively little has been written about the planning and management of student support services.

STUDIES ABROAD

Policies, Patterns and Growth

There have been several attempts in conducting studies on this area. Beardsley (1975), Pawdry (1975), Grimmett (1975), Kinsey (1975), Kuznestov (1975), Meirerhenry (1975), Wedemeyer (1975), Chamberlain (1977), Guiton (1977), Nolan (1977), Perry (1976), Pogano (1977), Sims (1978), Green (1980), Schuyer (1981) and Rumble and Borden (1983) are some of them. The common findings that have been marked in these studies are that the organisation structures are integrated within a larger system of education, usually a larger university complex. Within each education set-up, the systems follow certain overall policy statements on their roles and functions. The systems, however, have unique policy-making models.

Learners of the System

Needs and Aspirations of Learners

On the areas of needs and aspirations of learner for joining different courses, two types of studies have been conducted. One was at the stage previous to entrance to the courses before establishment of the institutions and the other was at the post-entrance stage.

In the pre-entry stage, in one case of one study in the open university, the UK, the target group learners were asked about their awareness of existence of the open university (Perry, 1976).

The study revealed that over five years (1971-76) in the UK 64 per cent of the total adult population had known about the university. From 1971 to 1976; the percentage of men being aware of the open university, increased from 33 per cent to 76 per cent and the percentage of women increased from 29 per cent to 58 per cent. Further, in the stage of inception of the same institution, a sample survey of 3000 adults revealed that 5 per cent of the total respondents were very much interested in joining the open university courses and 0.9 per cent respondents stated definitely to be amongst first applicants (Perry, 1976). In the case of few correspondence institutions in the UK and Japan the target group learners stated about different reasons for joining the courses, which can be placed under two clusters, such as:

(i) to improve upon academic qualifications, to continue with higher education, use of leisure time and to bring about personal development [Sorgel, 1966, Ministry of Education, Japan, 1975; and Wanieweicz (1981)]; and

(ii) to improve upon occupational efficiency to be placed in higher jobs, to bring about economic efficiency in terms of improvement of living condition (Sorgel, 1966, Wanieweicz, 1981 and McIntosh, 1978).

The studies of second category revealed that the students who had already entered the correspondence education stream had done so because of the above stated reasons (Childs, 1966; National Extension College, 1967; Fairbenks, 1971; Glatter and Wedell, 1971; McIntosh, 1978; Peters, 1978; Idle *et. al.*, 1978). Further, motivation for improvement of social status had prompted many students to join the courses (National Extension College, 1967 and McIntosh, 1978). In one of the studies of second category attempt was made to analyse the motivational factors of students on the basis of age and sex (Wanieweicz, 1981). The study revealed that job-related goals were the best motivating forces for most of the young men of 18 to 24 years and women of 25 to 44 years. The women of above 45 years age group stated that their joining was motivated by their hobbies, recreation and family concerns. However, it could be observed that factors like: (i) changing personal or family circumstances, and (ii) financial problems for unemployed ones had obstructed the ways of potential students to join the correspondence education programme (McIntosh, 1978).

Characteristics of Learners

Studies concerned with learners' characteristics can be recognised with several background variables like age, sex, marital status, regional background, employment, occupation, social class and academic qualification. Further, in some of the cases, analyses of learner's characteristics were done taking into consideration the courses inside the correspondence education system and the outside parallel systems. With regard to age of the students, it could be found that in the UK very high percentage of correspondence education students belonged to around 30 years of age (Glatter and Wedell, 1971; McIntosh, 1978) in the USA and West Germany around 55 to 56 percent correspondence students belonged to 35 years age group (Johnstone and Rivera, 1965; Peters, 1965) in Costa Rica very high percentage of students of distance university were below 25 years age group (Rumble and Borden, 1983). In comparison to other adult education course students, the correspondence course students were found to be quite younger (Johnstone and Rivera, 1965).

With regard to the sex of students of correspondence education, the studies conducted in the USA and the UK, revealed that most of the students i.e., around 70 per cent were men (Johnstone and Rivera, 1965; Glatter and Wedell, 1971). In the case of Open University, the U.K. the situation of 1971 i.e., 70 per cent men and 30 per cent women changed towards 56 percent men and 44 percent women by the year 1978 (McIntosh, 1978). In Canada, however, the largest percentage of students were women especially from 25 to 34 years age group (Waniewicz, 1981).

Regarding marital status of correspondence students it was found that most of them were married and had children (Meddleton, 1965; Schram, 1967; Short, 1967; Waniewicz, 1981), Glatter and Wedell, 1971; McIntosh, 1978; Rumbh and Borden, 1983.

About residences of students the studies like Peters (1965) and Glatter and Wadell (1971), revealed that in comparison to ruralites more urban-based learners were attracted towards correspondence system.

The studies on employment and occupation background of correspondence students revealed that among professional course students, 99 per cent were employed ones whereas in the case of general courses 69 per cent students were having employment (Glatter and Wedell, 1971). It was found in general that employed students were absorbed in several professions as civil servants, industrial workers, library servants, housewives, commerce and private sector-oriented professionals, clerical and office staff, administration and management personnel, shop-keepers, armed forces personnel, etc. (International Correspondence School, 1965, Glatter and Wedell, 1971; McIntosh, 1974).

The academic background of correspondence learners at university stage was found in varied forms. The open university of UK, which did not insist on formal schooling experiences had attracted one-third of its first batch students during 1971 from non-formal education background and the rest from formal background (McIntosh, 1974). In another study Perry (1976) it could be found that during 1971 only 33 per cent students of the open university were fulfilling the minimum qualification requirements for entry into other British Universities. However, by the year 1975 the students percentage from such category had increased to 46.4. The studies conducted in Minnesota University had revealed that the correspondence students grade points were higher than those of day scholars, evening course students and summer students (Kanun, 1968). However, the studies conducted by Meddleton (1965), Schrams (1967) and Short (1967) revealed different results i.e., the general correspondence students were often less able academically or less qualified than full time students taking similar courses.

STUDIES ON INSTRUCTIONAL SYSTEM OF DISTANCE EDUCATION

(i) Descriptive Studies

Studies under this category had aimed at description of

students participation in instructional programmes, their study habits, problems in studies, etc. In the open university of U.K. (McIntosh, 1974) the majority of students (70 per cent to 80 per cent) choose to watch and listen the instructional programmes broadcast at their leisure. Regarding use of study centres, it was found that in the early weeks many students (50 per cent to 60 per cent) attended them mainly to see counsellors and other students to familiarise themselves with the system. Later on, the attendants percentages receded to 30 per cent or so. As the examination approached, some students were unable to go to study centres. A study conducted by Graham (1971) on completion of assignments in Mermods revealed that 46 per cent students consulted their friends and family members and 45 per cent consulted available literature, and 18 per cent students left the tasks unresolved that they would have proceeded at the same pace with or without assignments. 21 per cent students expressed that studies would have been completed slowly without assignments, and 37 per cent students commented that assignments caused them complete the course more promptly. Very high percentage (71 per cent) of students called for more comprehensive assignments.

Any study conducted by Idle *et. al.* (1978) on study pattern of successful external students in Australia revealed that an average students studied about 8 hours per week per subject. There existed much differences due to the varying sizes of the subjects-based credit points. Regarding their schedule of study 70 per cent students reported that they follow a set schedule for study. It was found that the city dwellers scheduled their studies better than the country dwellers. Most of the students stated that the textbooks were main sources of information for them. The use of library materials by students depended on the nature of the subject and ready availability of material. Regarding audio cassettes, it could be found that the isolated students used them more often than metropolitan and country students.

(ii) Experimentation on Instructional Process

A few studies were conducted to study the efficiency of certain methods of instruction over others. Simich (1965) conducted a study of the comparative effectiveness of self-instructional methods of learning including PLM and correspondence courses techniques. It was found that the correspondence students out score the individualized instruction group but the difference in achievement scores was not significant. Willingham's (1971) study aimed at studying comparative effectiveness of combination of different groups of methods viz., (1) Students meeting the instructors who used lecture-*cum*-discussion approaches three times a week; (2) Students meeting tutors once in a week and taking correspondence study; (3) Students taking usual correspondence courses. No significant differences could be marked in the achievement of students who undertook these different methods of instruction. Green (1967) studied the effectiveness of correspondence study methods by using PLM, TV and home works/assignments. The methods were found to be equally effective in comparison to conventional methods of teaching, as there did not exist significant differences between the achievement scores of students undertaking studies through different methods.

Wilson's (1968) experimentation aimed at studying the effect of immediate feedback, planned review of lessons and voice components upon prompt response of assignments by the students and their achievement in examinations. It was found that the students included in the experimental group were somewhat more likely to start, more likely to complete and tried to complete the courses in lesser time. However, there was no additional effect upon the rate of sending assignments and achievement of those students in comparison with students of control group who took usual correspondence courses. Preiffer (1971) studied to determine the effect of letters and postcards of encouragement on rate of submission of assignments. It was found that neither the letters nor the postcards of encouragement resulted in a significant increase in the rate of submission of assignments.

(iii) Reaction of Students towards Instructional System

The reaction studies which included the responses of students entering the course, dropouts and students completing the courses indicated both positive as well as negative opinions about the instructional process of correspondence education.

Regarding efficiency of correspondence studies over regular studies, most of the students expressed a high opinion about the correspondence studies, provided, they included better quality exercises and test materials (Glatter and Wedell, 1971). On this matter most of the students completing the courses successfully commented similarly. However, they pointed out that better correspondence study depended upon regularly study of the texts, self-checking exercises followed by assignments and teachers evaluative remarks on them, etc. (Graham, 1971). Most of the students of correspondence courses opined that correspondence studies provided more effective exercise and test materials in comparison to part-time oral courses. Also, they were more helpful to assess students progress by themselves (Glatter and Wedell, 1971). While reacting to instructional system most of the dropouts stated that correspondence studies required more work and they lessened their interest in the absence of classroom contact (Sloan, 1966 and Pulley, 1971). However, in Pulley (1971)'s study most of the dropouts stated that the quality of correspondence studies were either superior or equal to other approaches of instruction.

Lockwood (1973) while reacting course evaluation instruments, the evaluations of 87 per cent to 97 per cent of the completers indicated the course:

(a) was equal to or better than comparable residence courses on campus,
(b) met an important need for the participants,
(c) could be learned effectively through correspondence study,
(d) recommended that additional correspondence courses of this type be developed. Nearly 42 per cent said they would take another correspondence course while 15 per cent said they would not.

Woolsey, Paul Warren (1974) on Evaluation of Correspondence Education found :

(a) Correspondence education is an effective method for individuals who possess the personal characteristics necessary for successful completion of correspondence course.

(b) Correspondence graduate can compete successfully for jobs in their area of study.

(c) Alternatives to the present evaluation procedures do exist, and include accreditation by the National Home Study Council and evaluation by an agency such as CASE.

(d) Present procedures used to qualify to sit for such examinations test for individuals background rather than his job, knowledge and skills.

Robert Mike (1978) in his study on open systems' approach to professional education, revealed an adequately designed model, a high degree of openness, a performances-oriented curriculum and student support systems, as well as an objective based instructional system.

Carpenter (1981) attempted to study the significant difference between completers and non-completers of correspondence courses in self-actualizing levels.

(a) It was concluded that completion of correspondence courses did not provide a good indicator of self-direction in learning for the population utilized in this study, some of which could not be adequately met through completion of highly structured correspondence courses. Therefore, no conclusions concerning the relationship of self-direction in learning and self-actualization could be drawn from this study.

(b) The findings suggested that the needs of adult learners who enroll in university correspondence study for non-credit reasons are not being fully met under the present structure of rigid requirements and limited course content.

Robinson has set out basic elements of student support, drawn largely on the practice of the Open University UK (Robinson, 1981). Paul & Rumble have addressed the area of student support within more general work on management of Distance Education (Paul, 1990, Rumble, 1992); the latter has also examined student support from the perspective of the economics of Distance Education (Rumble, 1997). Sewart has more specifically addressed the development of support to students within a service industry framework (Sewart, 1993), and there are a number of essays on management of student support in Distance Education, in particular in the context of dual mode institutions, in Mills & Tait (1997). Brindley has discussed the contextual criteria which are key to designing student support services and the outcomes of persistence and attrition (Brindley, 1995). The most extended review of the field has been produced by Sweet (1993) for the Commonwealth of Learning, in a volume that has a most helpful bibliography, while recent case studies and accompanying analysis have came from South Africa (Nonyongo and Ngengebule, 1998; SAIDE, 2000).

The above review of researches shows that the area of student support services of conventional university and open university is a comparatively fresh area of research. It is therefore, apparent that Student Support Service specific to conventional universities has not been investigated as yet to the best knowledge of the researcher. The present study therefore is expected to fill this existing gap and throw light on the areas needed for planning better support services.

The study aims to build on a range of work in a practical way in order to identify the principles of planning for the development of student support services especially in dual mode universities at a time of great change. It is intended that a flexible framework of ideas and models will be developed, which will provide a basis for work in dual mode universities. This in turn will certainly yield findings of significant implications.

3

Study Methodology

3.1 INTRODUCTION

Research design is a blue print of the proposed study which details the salient features of the envisaged research in terms of procedure, tools & techniques. The review of related literature presented in previous chapter enabled the choosing of the method of investigation for this study and in the construction of the tools for gathering data.

This chapter delineates the research design adopted for the present investigation. The main themes of this chapter revolves round the method used for investigation, nature and size of the sample selected for investigation tools used for collection of data, method of data collection, coding and statistical techniques employed for analysis and interpretation of data. This chapter also gives a brief profile of the selection of institutions for the study.

3.2 SELECTION OF INSTITUTIONS FOR THE STUDY

The Institute of Distance Education of University of

Mumbai, a conventional university is one of the oldest in the State of Maharashtra and the Indira Gandhi National Open University, New Delhi being the only national open university and having its study centres at Mumbai are the two institutions selected for the present investigation. The association of the researcher with these institutions were other factors for selection. The following are the brief profiles of the two institutions.

3.2.1 University of Mumbai

The University of Mumbai (known earlier as university of Bombay) is one of the oldest and premier universities in India. It was established in 1857 consequent upon "Woods Education Despatch".

The profile of this university carved out in 145 years of its functioning attests to its manifold achievements as the intellectual and moral powerhouse of the society. The university has always given best to the country in general and to the city of Mumbai in particular by enthusiastically shouldering an ever growing load of responsibilities and challenges emanating from changing social values and opportunities.

The clarion call given to the first eight graduates of the University on 28th April, 1862 by Sir Bartle Frere, the Chancellor of University of Bombay exhorted them to restore the pristine vigour in a society that was plauged by disorder and intellectual stagnation. Indeed, it was a massive task to awaken the society that was deep in its slumber.

In 1863, the gates of the University were laid open to women who were thus far denied enlightenment through education.

The Indian Universities Act, 1904, enabled the Bombay University to exercise greater control over teaching through the provisions of conditions of affiliation, periodic inspection, submission of reports and returns by colleges. The independence of the country led to the re-organisation of functions and powers of the university with the passing of the Bombay University Act, 1953. Further, with the advent of other universities in the state, there was need for providing a uniform legislation for the governance of various universities in the state of Maharashtra. Accordingly the Maharashtra Act of 1974 was passed. To meet the long felt necessities of the ensuing 21st century, the Maharashtra Universities Act, 1994 was passed for non-agricultural and non-technological universities in the state of Maharashtra.

The University has been accredited at the 5 Star level (highest grade) by the National Assessment and Accreditation Council, Bangalore, and is now a University with potential for excellence by UGC. It is rated among the top 500 Universities of the world.

Organisational Structure
University of Mumbai

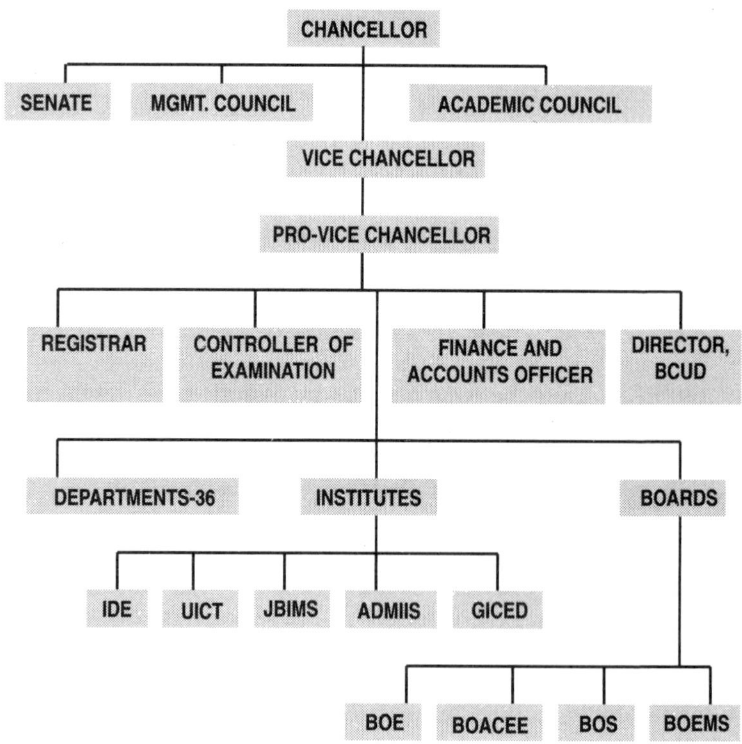

Statistical Profile

The jurisdiction of university extends over Greater Mumbai, and the districts of Thane, Raigad, Ratnagiri and

Sindhudurg. It has 36 Departments with a student enrolment of about 7,700. Presently 510 colleges are affiliated to it having a student enrolment of 5,05,000. There are 4,500 students registered for the Post-Graduate degrees in the 67 institutions recognised by the University. The number of examinations conducted by the University is 938.

3.2.2 Institute of Distance Education

The Syndicate of the University of Mumbai at its meeting held on 26th September, 1970, considered proposal made by Shri A.N. Namjoshi, a member of the Syndicate, that the possibility of *introducing* correspondence courses and external degree courses in the university for the benefit of a large number of students who cannot avail themselves of the facilities of morning/evening classes be explored. The suggestion was referred by the syndicate to the Academic Council and the Council at its meeting held on 24th March, 1971, approved the report of its committee and recommended to the syndicate that the courses be started from June 1971.

The correspondence courses were then introduced in the University with a nomenclature as "The Directorate of Correspondence Courses" for which correspondence instructions were to be given at the first year Arts and first year Commerce examination to be held in the first half of the year 1972. Initially, it started with a meagre registration of 845 students which has grown up to a staggering figure of about 71,000 students during 2008-09.

The Directorate of Correspondence Courses was up-graded as "Directorate of Distance Education in the year 1985 and the full time Director was appointed by the University. With the upgradation, the jurisdiction was extended to cover the entire country. Earlier, the enrolment was restricted to persons residing within the university area. Consequent upon the assent accorded by the Chancellor to the Statute 504, A to G the Directorate of Distance Education has been designated as the Institute of Distance Education by a notification issued by the Registrar on 2nd June 1993. It is now likely to be Institute of Distance and Open Learning (IDOL).

Special Features

1. Eligibility requirements, curricular content, mode of examination and the award of degrees are on par with the colleges affiliated to the University of Mumbai and the Departments of the University.
2. Printed study material in English and wherever possible in Marathi.
3. Personal Contact Classes are arranged in some of the subjects during evening hours/Sundays/Holidays in the city of Mumbai and around for guidance of the students.
4. Audio-Visual Centre/Library/Reading Room facility in Mumbai.
5. Home-lending of books against deposit.

Important Achievements

The Institute is presently located in its own building of about 77,000 square feet area and having a separate library exclusively for the distance learners with more than 35,000 books. Some of the students have topped the merit list of the University and have bagged Gold Medal in M.A. Sanskrit, M.A. Marathi and Chancellor's Medal in M.A. Hindi. 116 students of IDE have gone abroad for seeking higher education in USA, UK, Australia, Canada, New Zealand, etc. during last year. So far as the academic performance of the students is concerned, there were a good number of students who secured first class at B.A., B.Com., M.A. and M.Com. degree examinations last year.

Instructional System

The Methodology of instruction at Institute of Distance Education of the University of Mumbai is different from that of the conventional university/college. The system is more learner-oriented and the learner is an active participant in the teaching-learning process.

The instructional system of IDE comprises :

- Printed study materials are in English and Marathi.
- Supporting Audio-Video Programmes. (Curriculum-

based Video Cassettes in some subjects for Undergraduate and Post-graduate students).

- Face to face interaction with teachers at PCP centres and also at Headquarters.
- Counselling at Headquarters by the core faculty.

Student Support Services

(i) Personal Contact Programme

The Institute organises personal contact programmes in certain subjects in Mumbai for the benefit of students, in the evening from 6.00 p.m. to 8.00 p.m. or sometimes on Sundays/ Holidays. Through the lectures are not compulsory, it is an attempt to provide guidance to students in solving their academic difficulties.

(ii) Library Facilities

IDE has a well-equipped library consisting of good collection of around 35,000 books on various subjects of study like Economics, Politics, Education, Psychology, Philosophy, Sociology, History, Accounts, Management Mathematics and Literature in Marathi, Hindi & English languages, etc. The textbooks for further reading mentioned in the Study Material/ Syllabus are available in the library for reading.

The Library has built a special collection of reference books like Encyclopaedias, Dictionaries of languages and subject Dictionaries, Directories, Yearbooks in various disciplines of knowledge.

The Library offers the following services to the IDE students :

Reading Room Facility—Only IDE students can use the Reading Hall facility for their studies both in the IDE Building. at Vidyanagari, Santacruz (East) and the Vidyapeeth Vidyarthi Bhavan building, Churchgate, Mumbai-400 020. The Reading Room remains open from 8.00 a.m. to 8.00 p.m. on working days (Monday to Saturday) except on 2nd and 4th Monday.

Home Lending of Books Facility—Students may avail of this facility of taking a book at home for their studies by paying Rs. 200 deposit.

Referring Question Papers and Syllabus—Students may obtain question papers of last two years and syllabus for reference in the library. Photocopying facility is also available.

(iii) Audio-Video Centre

Some curriculum-based Audio & Vido cassettes in the subjects of Economics, Commerce, Education, Sociology, etc. are available in the Audio-Video cente of the IDE.

3.2.3 Indira Gandhi National Open University

The Indira Gandhi National Open University was established by an Act of Parliament in 1985. Today it serves the educational aspirations of about 1.8 million students through 21 Schools of Studies and an elaborate network of 62 regional centres, 2053 study centres, 51 partner institutions spread across the country, and a number of overseas centres. The University is making all efforts to take higher education to the doorsteps of the hitherto unreached. Apart from teaching and research, extension and training form the mainstay of its academic activities. It also acts as a national resource centre; and more importantly, functions as an apex body to promote and maintain standards of distance education. The Commonwealth of Learning has recognised it as one of its centres of excellence.

Objectives

In order to fulfil the vision of democratising higher education and providing access to all segments of people, the University is mandated to :

- impart education and knowledge through various flexible means suited to the open and distance education mode;
- provide higher education to large sections of population, particularly the disadvantages segments of the society;
- promote higher education to large sections of population, particularly the disadvantaged segments of the society; and

- encourage, coordinate and assist open universities and distance learning systems to uphold standards in such systems.

Organisational Structure

The President of India is the Visitor of the University and the Board of Management is the highest decision-making body of the University. The Academic Council, the Planning Board, the Finance Committee, and the Distance Education Council are statutory authorities of the University. Each of the nine School of Studies, is headed by a Director; and compirses a few Discipline Groups, coordinated by a Discipline Coordinator. There are fifteen divisions to provide support to and facilitate the work of School of Studies. Some divisions directly serve the distance learners. While the Vice Chancellor is assisted by the pro-Vice-Chancellors, the Registrar looks after the administrative matters, and the Finance Officer takes care of the financial matters relating to the entire university operation within the country and overseas. The Schools of Studies enjoy considerable autonomy in the design and development of academic, training, research and extension programmes. While IGNOU acts as an open university in so far as it offers academic programmes, it is also mandated by the Indian Parliament to act as an apex body to coordinate and maintain standards in the distance education systems in the country.

Unique Features

The University offers a large number of need-based programmes and courses through multi-channels of learning with the learner at the focus. Some of the unique features of the system are :

Need-Based Academic Programmes

The University offers 167 academic programmes, comprising 1600 courses, that are need-based, unconventional, and vocation-oriented with a focus on socio-economic development. The programmes are at the awareness, certificate, diploma, degree (Bachelor's, Master's and Doctoral) levels.

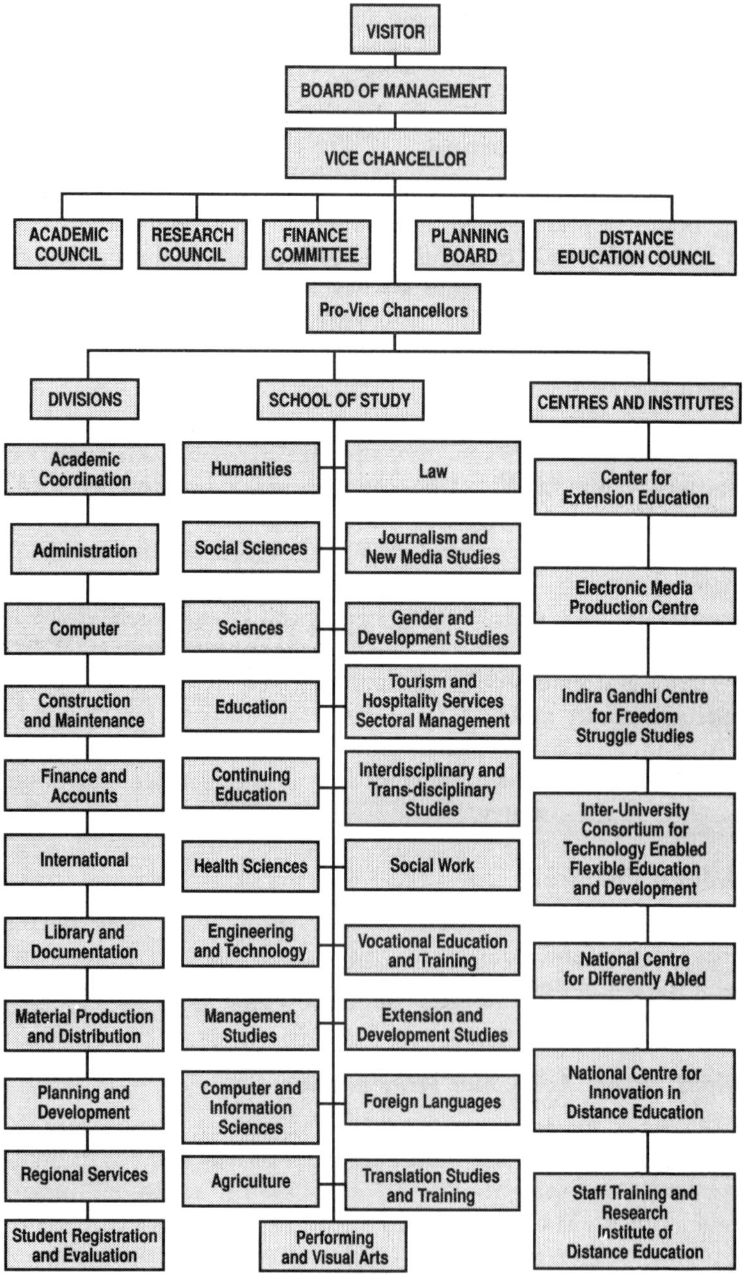
VISITOR
BOARD OF MANAGEMENT
VICE CHANCELLOR
ACADEMIC COUNCIL
RESEARCH COUNCIL
FINANCE COMMITTEE
PLANNING BOARD
DISTANCE EDUCATION COUNCIL
Pro-Vice Chancellors
DIVISIONS
Academic Coordination
Administration
Computer
Construction and Maintenance
Finance and Accounts
International
Library and Documentation
Material Production and Distribution
Planning and Development
Regional Services
Student Registration and Evaluation
SCHOOL OF STUDY
Humanities
Law
Social Sciences
Journalism and New Media Studies
Sciences
Gender and Development Studies
Education
Tourism and Hospitality Services Sectoral Management
Continuing Education
Interdisciplinary and Trans-disciplinary Studies
Health Sciences
Social Work
Engineering and Technology
Vocational Education and Training
Management Studies
Extension and Development Studies
Computer and Information Sciences
Foreign Languages
Agriculture
Translation Studies and Training
Performing and Visual Arts
CENTRES AND INSTITUTES
Center for Extension Education
Electronic Media Production Centre
Indira Gandhi Centre for Freedom Struggle Studies
Inter-University Consortium for Technology Enabled Flexible Education and Development
National Centre for Differently Abled
National Centre for Innovation in Distance Education
Staff Training and Research Institute of Distance Education

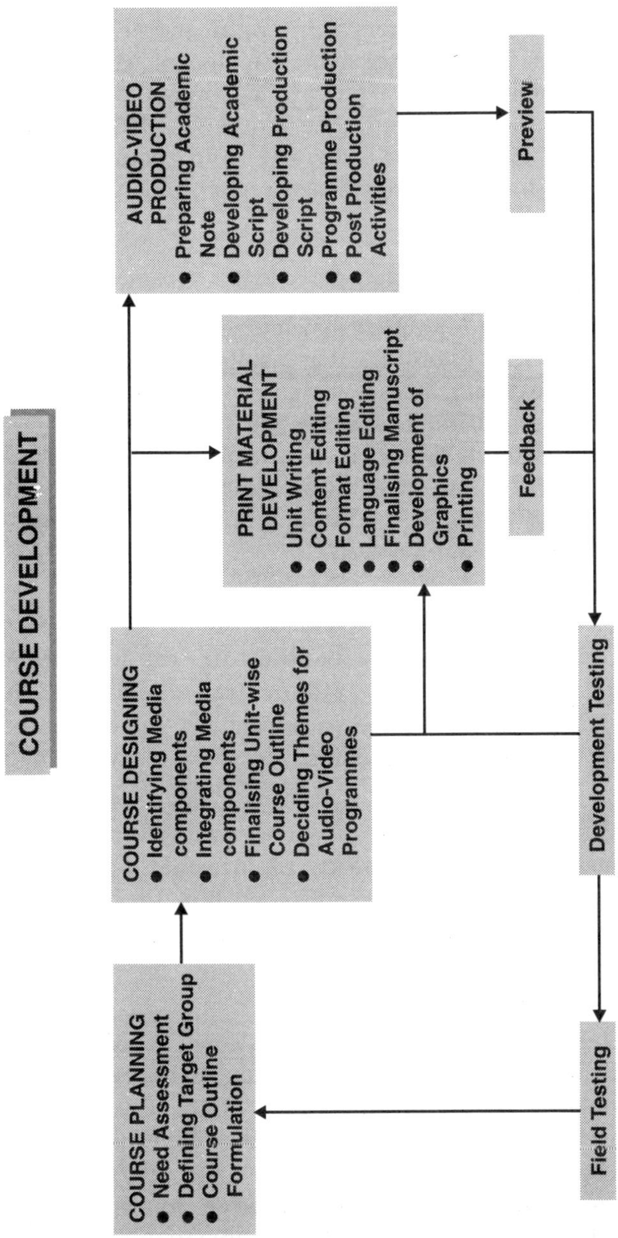
COURSE DEVELOPMENT
COURSE PLANNING
• Need Assessment
• Defining Target Group
• Course Outline Formulation
COURSE DESIGNING
• Identifying Media components
• Integrating Media components
• Finalising Unit-wise Course Outline
• Deciding Themes for Audio-Video Programmes
PRINT MATERIAL DEVELOPMENT
• Unit Writing
• Content Editing
• Format Editing
• Language Editing
• Finalising Manuscript
• Development of Graphics
• Printing
AUDIO-VIDEO PRODUCTION
• Preparing Academic Note
• Developing Academic Script
• Developing Production Script
• Programme Production
• Post Production Activities
Preview
Feedback
Development Testing
Field Testing

Diversified Learner Groups

IGNOU caters to learners from rural and tribal areas, disability groups, jails and rehabilitation houses, government and non-government sectors, parents and home-makers, the employers and the employed. The University has adopted special focus on women, socially and economically disadvantaged groups, the north-east region and other tribal areas of the country.

Rigorous Course Development

The procedures adopted for development of various multi-media learning packages are aimed at maintaining the quality of learning. The university follows a rigorous course design and development procedure, based on the principles of good practices in curriculum development and instructional design. IGNOU utilises the expertise available in-house and with international and national institutions and non-government organisations in the team-approach.

Multi-Channel Learning

The University provides a multi-media learning system comprising print, audio, video, radio, television, teleconferencing, interactive radio counselling, Internet-based learning and face-to-face counselling.

On-line Learning

To meet the emerging needs of information era, the University offers some programmes on-line through tele-learning centres within its virtual campus initiatives.

Credit System and Modularity

The University follows the credit system whereby each course and programme has a specified number of credits. Each credit involves 30 hours of study time of the learners. The learners can accumulate credits as per their convenience. The University has also adopted the modular approach, that helps the learners in moving gradually, through small modules, towards higher levels of learning. The combination of modules leads to certificate, diploma and degree programmes in an area of study.

Flexible and Individualised Learning

In tune with the nature of the open learning system, the University offers a lot of flexibility and openness to the learners in terms of :

- Eligibility and admission procedures
- Place of study
- Pace and duration of study

Student Support Network

The University provides effective student support services through a network of :

- 62 Regional Centres located in the capital city of almost every state.
- 17 Recognised Regional Centres catering to Army, Air Force and Navy personnel. These Centres operate under single window system.
- 2053 Study Centres, work and programme centres, and partner institutions spread across the country. At the study centres, the learners are provided the services in respect of: subject-specific academic-counselling, audio and video viewing, library facilities, teleconferencing information services related to rules, regulations, counselling and examination schedules of the university, assignment submission, evaluation and feedback, term-end examinations, computer access, laboratory work and other practicles.

Nearly 21,000 academic peers from various disciplines of the conventional University system are involved in these operations. IGNOU has established a *Student Welfare Cell* located at the vice chancellor's office to respond to the problems of its learners. The Student Services Centre at the headquarters and regional centres report to the cell.

LEARNING SYSTEM

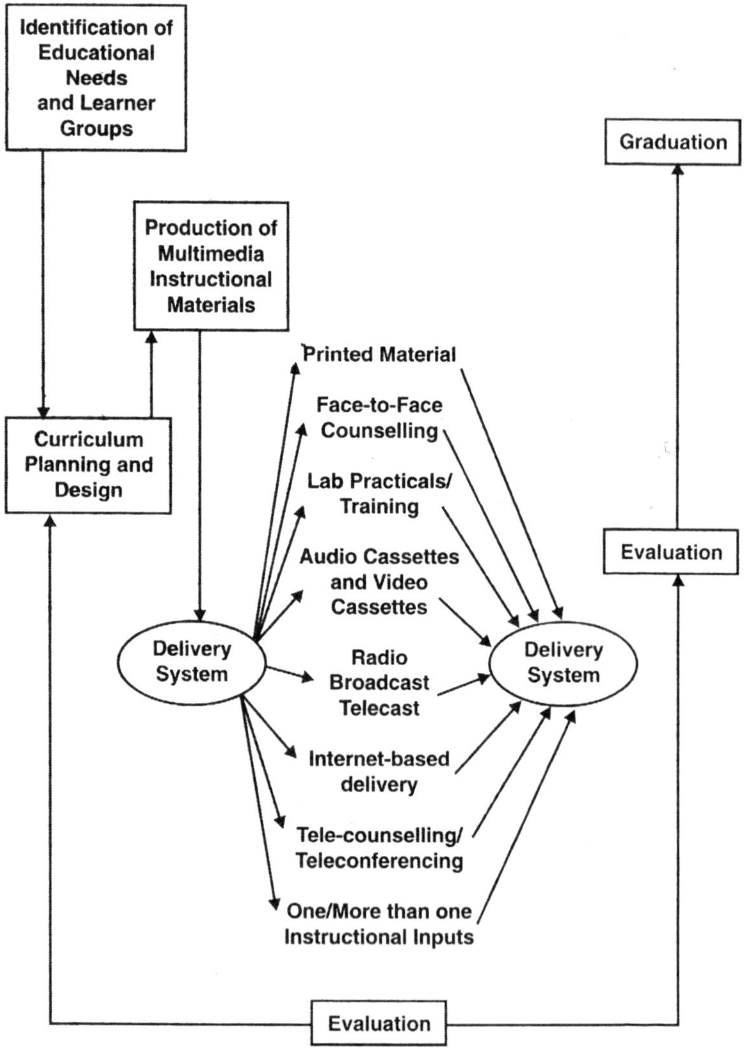

In areas where study centres are not available, the innovative concept of the Distance Learning Facilitators (DLF) has been put in place. A DLF is an effective mechanism to untilise educated and trained human resources to provide support to our students.

Multilingual Instructional Packages

Most programmes and courses offered by IGNOU are available in English and Hindi. In addition, a number of courses are also being offered in a number of Indian Languages by the university.

Academic Programmes

Unlike the conventional system, distance education involves team teaching where a host of specialists are involved in the design, development, delivery and evaluation of multi-media self-learning materials. The University offers 167 academic programmes comprising 1600 courses at certificate, diploma and degree levels. In addition, a number of non-accredited extension and skill-oriented programmes are offered through the Centre for Extension Education.

While STRIDE and EMPC are involved in providing design, training and media support to the School and Studies, they have also developed programmes which are offered through School of Studies.

Electronic Media

Reaching a large number of students and further enriching/explaining the study materials have been the major objectives of audio, video, radio, television, radio counselling, teleconferencing, and the like. The University has a state-of-the-art Electronic Media Production Centre (EMPC). The following media resources are available in the University:

- *Regular two-way audio and one-way video teleconferencing*: About 250 interactive nodes spread all over the country offer two-way interactive tele-counselling, tele-teaching, tele-training, tele-discussion and extended contact programme. The facility has gone digital and is now available through INSAT-3B.
- *Interactive radio counselling* : This facility is being offered to bridge the gap between the institution and the learners through instant response to their academic and administrative queries. Now, 184 radio stations

across the country broadcast interactive phone-in counselling every Sunday (4.00-5.00 p.m.). The students participate from their homes through toll-free telephone to interact with the experts at various AIR studios.

- *Gyan Darshan* : A full television channel for education broadcasts programmes for 24 hours. The programmes are available through cable network of local cable operators, and are contributed by IGNOU, UGC-CFC, NCERT, CIET, NOS, NLM and some government and non-government organisations.
- Gyan Vani is a radio cooperative, devoted exclusively to education and development through regional production and broadcasting.

Material Production and Delivery

Except a few on-line courses for which the course materials are available on the Internet, materials for all other programmes are despatched through post. In the year 2000-01, nearly 0.65 million packets were despatched to students. The University also makes its materials available to all others interested through a chain of private booksellers and its own marketing cell located in the MPDD.

Student Evaluation

In IGNOU, continuous evaluation and feedback to students form an integral part of evaluation and certification. Student evaluation is in the form of evaluation of tutor-marked and computer-marked assignment—responses, projects, term-end examination scripts, etc. The weightage of continuous component varies in the range 20-30% and the term-end component carries 70-80% weightage. The University conducts term-end examination through a network of examination centres spread across the length and breadth of the country. In the twelfth Convocation of the University held in 2001, 62,369 students were awarded certificates, diplomas and degrees.

3.3 THE METHOD

The word 'Survey' means 'to view comprehensively and in detail' and in another sense it refers specifically to the act of 'obtaining data for mapping'. Survey has emerged as one of the most popular and common place approaches to social research. The survey approach is a research strategy and researchers who adopt the strategy are able to use a whole range of methods within the strategy: questionnaires, interviews, documents and observation.

The term 'normative' implies the determination of normal or typical conditions, facts or practices. The term normative survey is generally used for the type of research, which proposes to ascertain what is the normal or typical condition or practice at the present time. The survey type of research is often confused with the mere gathering and tabulating the data while it goes beyond this. What is distinctive about the survey is its combination of a commitment to a breadth of study, a focus on the snapshot at a given point in time and a dependence on empirical data. According to Best, "The Survey is an important type of study. It must not be confused with the mere clerical routine of gathering and tabulating figures. It involves a clearly defined problem and definite objectives. It requires expert and imaginative planning, careful analysis and interpretation of the data gathered and logical and skillful reporting of the findings". (Best, 1978).

In order to achieve the objectives of the present study normative or survey or descriptive research method was used for investigation, as this was found to be the most appropriate method to survey the current practices of student support services, prevailing in the Conventional University as well as Open University. Qualitative research has its own special approach to the collection and analysis of data, which marks it out as quite different from its quantitative counterpart. Qualitative research deals with small numbers of instances to be researched. In the present study qualitative research was also used as the basis for generating models, and theories based upon the practices of Student Support Services prevalent in the Open University of United Kingdom and European Association of Distance Teaching University.

3.4 THE POPULATION

A population may refer to all of any specified groups of human being or of non-human entities such as objects, geographical areas, time units, methods, test or institutes. The population selected for the present investigation is the distance learners who are undergoing Bachelor's Degree Programme of the Institute of Distance Education of University of Mumbai and Indira Gandhi National Open University, Mumbai during the period 2001-02. (January to May 2002).

As per the address list obtained from the Institute of Distance Education and IGNOU study centres, Mumbai there were 2547 and 153 students respectively enrolled in the second year B.A. course during the period 2001-02 which constitute the population for this study.

Once the population is defined for the study the next step is to select a representative sample from the population. It has been discussed in the following paragraphs.

3.5 THE SAMPLE

Social researchers are frequently faced with the fact that they cannot collect data from everyone who is in the category being researched. As a result they rely on getting evidence from a portion of the whole in the expectation and hope that what is found in that portion applies equally to the rest of the population.

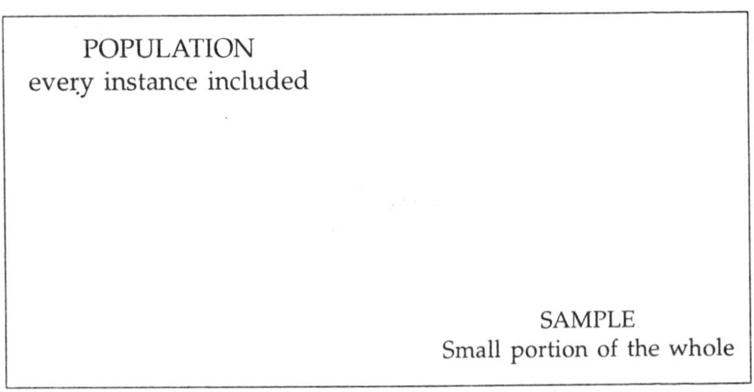

Probability sampling is based on the idea that the people or events that are chosen as the sample are chosen because the researcher has some notion of the probability that these will be a representative cross-section of people or events in the whole population being studied.

Systematic sampling a variant probability sampling was used for drawing the sample of distance learners and they were sent questionnaires by post with a self-addressed stamped envelope for reply.

Since the researcher is familiar to the distance learners of both the institute and the nature of topic has some bearings on the distance learners, it was hoped that there will be good response to the questionnaire sent by post. Although the proportion of people who responded to the postal questionnaires was 22.3 percentage this will still provide sufficient data for analysis.

The final sample for the present study consist of 120 distance learners of IDE, and 56 distance learners of IGNOU. The sampling frame is summarized below in Table 3.1

TABLE 3.1
Sampling Frame

University Type	*Total No. of Distance learners (Population)*	*Total No. of D.L. sent questionnaire by post*	*Response received*
Conventional University	2547	637 (25.0%)	120 (18.8%)
Open University	153	153 (100%)	56 (36.6%)
Total	2700	790 (29.25%)	176 (22.3%)

3.6 DESCRIPTION OF TOOLS

The selection of suitable instruments or tools is of vital importance for successful research. Questionnaire is defined as "A systematic compilation of questions that are submitted to a sampling of population from which information is desired".

Questionnaire falls under data gathering devices which make use of properly prepared forms for inquiring into and securing information about certain phenomenon under study. Generally the word 'questionnaire' refers to a device for securing answers to questions by using a form which the respondent fills in himself. Questionnaire is a simple and clear form to get objective results in the best possible way.

The present study has been undertaken by adopting the questionnaire method. Two sets of questionnaires were used to collect data and information for achieving the objectives of the study. They are :

(a) Questionnaire for Director/Coordinator.
(b) Questionnaire for Students.

3.6.1 Questionnaire for Director/Coordinator

It is a very comprehensive questionnaire; meant for eliciting information and data about the prevailing practices of student support services from the Director/Coordinator of the institute.

The covering letter accompanying the questionnaire contains some information about the purposes and significance of the study and a request for co-operating in the successful completion of the study.

The questionnaire was pilot tested by five experts in the field of distance education who were sent the questionnaire along with the objectives of the study. It was also presented before the research committee of YCMOU for their comments/ suggestion. Finally 60 questions were selected which form the basis of questionnaire for Director/Coordinator. The questionnaire is very extensive, therefore demands greater effort on the part of those responding.

The questions refer to the following four components of Student Support Services:

a – Study material,
b – Assignment,
c – Personal Contact Programme, and
d – Study centre.

There are 20 questions on study materials beginning with question numbers 1 to 20; 11 questions on assignment from question numbers 21 to 31; 07 questions on Personal Contact Programme from questions 32 to 38; 09 questions on Study Centres from questions 39 to 47 and 13 questions on some other Support Systems from questions 48 to 60. The details of the questions for Director/Coordinator is presented in Table 3.2.

TABLE 3.2
Component-wise No. of Questions for Director and Coordinator

Components of S.S.S.	*No. of Questions asked*	*Serial No. of Questions*
Study Material	20	1 – 20
Assignment	11	21 – 31
Personal Contact Programme	07	32 – 38
Study Centre	09	39 – 47
Other Support Systems	13	48 – 60

3.6.2 Questionnaire for Students

In order to get students reactions and opinions about the quality of study materials, suitability of assignment response sheets, convenience of personal contact programme lectures and the facilities available at the study centre, feedback devices and other support services provided by the institute, the questionnaire for students was developed. The questionnaire was basically designed to yield data that could be used as feedback from the students to critically study and assess the existing Student Support Services.

It is a very comprehensive questionnaire having 60 questions, thus requiring a great effort on the part of the responding students. Depending upon the nature of information required free response questions have also been included, particularly when suggestions are invited. In a few questions the respondent has to supply information while in some other he is required to select 'yes' or 'no' or rank the order.

Since the questionnaire for students was mailed, the title page of the questionnaire has been designed in the manner of 'Total Design Method' (TDM), (Dilman, 1987): it contains the theme of the study alongwith a covering letter, highlighting the significance of the study and requesting the student to return the duly filled questionnaire in the enclosed self-addressed stamped envelope.

The questionnaire for students, like the one for Director/ Coordinator was pilot tested and presented before the research committee of YCMOU after which the present questionnaire was finalised.

The questions seeking opinion of the students and their reactions to the four components of Student Support Services such as :

a – Study material.
b – Assignment.
c – Personal contact programme.
d – Study centre.

were tested in the questionnaire meant for students.

In the questionnaire the first 21 questions seek opinion of the students regarding study materials from question number 1 to 21, 13 questions as assignment from 22-34, 12 questions on personal contact programme from 35-46; and 14 questions on study centre from 47 to 60. The details of the questionnaire for students is presented in Table 3.3.

TABLE 3.3
Questionnaire for Students

Components of S.S.S.	*No. of Questions asked*	*Serial No. of Questions*
Study Material	21	1 – 20
Assignment	13	22 – 34
Personal Contact Programme	12	35 – 46
Study Centre	14	47 – 60

3.7 PROCEDURE OF DATA COLLECTION

Two types of data were required to achieve the objectives of the study, i.e. the institutional data from the Institute of

Distance Education of University of Mumbai and study centre of IGNOU, and the student's feedback data to elicit their opinion and suggestion and about Student Support Services.

The institutional data were collected personally by visiting the institute and the study centres of IGNOU, after seeking prior appointment with the Director and the Coordinator. After establishing rapport and explaining the purpose of the study in detail, the questionnaire for Director/Coordinator was administered.

This procedure ensured :

1. Uniform interpretation of the question, as doubts could be removed.
2. Quick return of the questionnaire with full information, i.e. no questions were left unanswered.
3. The reliability and validity of the information supplied in response to the questionnaire as the response of the Director/Coordinator were compared and cross-validated in some cases against the responses of the students with regard to the provision of Student Support Services made by the institute. A sample of comments on the students assignments official documents pertaining to the organization of PCP's and students participation in them, facilities and access to them in the study centres, quality of study materials were physically checked and verified as the researcher made personal visits to the institute and the study centres.

The questionnaire for the student was collected by mailing the questionnaire in the addresses obtained from the institute and study centres to the sample of students population. In order to ensure return, a self-addressed postage paid envelope accompanied the questionnaire sent to each student.

Thirty-two of the 790 addresses could not be delivered the questionnaire as they came back since the addresses have either changed or left the place. Therefore, addresses of another 32 students were drawn randomly and questionnaires were sent to them.

The Response Rate

Postal questionnaires are usually, though not always, received 'cold' by the respondents. This is mainly because there is not usually any personal contact between the researcher and the respondent and the respondent receives no prior notification of the arrival of the questionnaire. The proportion of people who respond as requested to such postal questionnaires is quite low. The actual proportion will depend on the nature of the topic, preoccupation of employed and married students in jobs, etc. As a rough guide, any social researcher will be lucky to get as many as 20 percent of the questionnaires returned (Denscombe, 1999)

However, a total of 150 filled questionnaires were returned in the first instance within a period of which ranged from 10-20 days. Having waited for a month, a reminder was sent to the students who did not respond. Another 26 students returned the filled questionnaires in response to the remainder. Thus, a total of 176 questionnaires were received and an overall response rate of 22.3 percent was achieved.

For a mailed questionnaire, an overall response rate of 20 percent can be considered quite satisfactory, particularly in the light that it does not vary too much over institutions. However, a note of caution about the representatives of the results is that the size of the final sample is just 176 students. Hence, the results pertaining to the students questionnaire, be interpreted in this light.

3.8 STATISTICAL TECHNIQUES USED

The present study utilises simple statistical techniques such as frequency and percentage. In addition, most of the data were interpreted through the method of descriptive analysis and wherever necessary cross-tabulations have been generated.

4

Student Support Services and Distance Education : An Analysis

4.1 INTRODUCTION

The present chapter has been devoted to the analysis and interpretation of the data in the context of the objectives and the research questions posed in the study.

In pursuance of the objectives of the study the obtained data were tabulated, classified and analysed to yield meaningful interpretation of results which may eventually lead to significant findings of the study. The data were literally analysed and interpreted with reference to the theories and ideas, issues and problems that were noted earlier as providing the context in which the research was conceived. The research makes sense of the findings by considering their implications beyond the confines of the current research. The analysis and interpretation of the results of the study have been presented in four parts.

In the first part the present practices of Student Support Services provided in the Distance Education Institute as well as Open University have been examined and interpreted through the questionnaire administered to the Director and Coordinator and the observation of the researcher. Further the questionnaire has been analysed taking into consideration the four components of the Student Support Services, i.e. Study Material, Assignment, Personal Contact Programme and Study Centre.

In the second part perception of the students and the provision of Student Support Services as viewed by the students have been critically examined through the students questionnaire administered on them. Students' reactions to the provisions made by the institutes have been analysed based upon the four components of the Student Support Services, i.e. Study Material, Assignment, Personal Contact Programme and Study Centre.

Part three provides for the study of the practices of Student Support Services as is obtained from the United Kingdom Open University (UKOU) and European Association of Distance Teaching Universities (EADTU). These two are acclaimed to be world leaders in Open and Distance Learning. Attempt has been made to see possible implications of these practices in the Indian context especially in a conventional set-up.

The fourth and the last part of analysis attempts to compare the existing Student Support Services of the Conventional University with that of the Open University and suggests the various ways of enhancing and improving the Student Support Services in the Conventional University.

PART ONE

4.2 PRACTICES OF STUDENT SUPPORT SERVICES

This part examines the prevailing practices of Student Support Services in the conventional University as well as Open University. This part caters to the first objective and research question of the study which are stated below—*OBJECTIVE 1.*

"To study the present practices adopted for Student Support Service in Distance Education Institute of Conventional University and Open University with respect to :

a — Study Material,
b — Assigment,
c — Personal Contact Prgramme, and
d — Study center.

Research Question 1

What provisions are made for providing Student Support Services to the Students of Distance Education Institute of conventional University and Open University?

In this section the providers of Student Support Services which include the Director and the Coordinator of the Institute Distance Education and Open University were administered questionnaire eliciting information about the present practices of Student Support Services adopted by their institutes. The analysis are presented below with regard to the four components of Student Support Services namely: (i) Study material, (ii) Assignment, (iii) Personal Contact Programme, and (iv) Study Centre.

4.2.1 Study Material

Printed Study Material is the backbone of any distance education programme. The quality and didactic suitability of these materials for independent/self-learning not only enhances students learning, but also determines the academic credibility of distance education. What constitute the course materials? How are they prepared ? How are they dispatched to students? These are some of the questions addressed to in this section Constitution of Study Materials bold.

With respect to the constitution of study materials and the media used them, the following facts emerged from the data and the observation of the researcher in these institutes. Study Materials of OU constituted of booklets of reading materials in Self Learning Instructional Material (SIM) format supported by audio and video cassettes in each course. Study Material of each course is supplemented by at least 4 video cassettes and 6 audio cassettes, thus making the learning truly multimedia. OU does not offer any course in which they have not prepared study materials. On the other hand in DEI the Study Material is in the format of text books and not written in self-instructional format style. Study material is not supplemented by audio-video cassettes. DEI also offers some courses in which study materials are not provided. It is the responsibility of the students to manage their study. Implication of this finding is that while UGC and DEC insists on developing courses with adequate study materials in self-learning format, DEI should prepare study materials in all the courses on offer and it should be in self-instructional format. It has also been observed that a beginning has been made in this direction in DEI in developing study materials in SIM mode.

Regarding size of the study materials, OUs Study materials are prepared in Blocks. A block normally contains three to five study units. A few blocks combined together make a course. Usually a block presents a content worth one credit (30 hours of study) and contains around sixty A4 size printed pages. This becomes handy for the students to refer. In DEI the study material is in text book format and each course is having one booklet consisting of about 150 to 200 pages.

Preparation of Study Materials

No task in distance education is as important and challenging as the writing and preparation of study materials. Different systems have been adopted for the preparation and development of study materials. The "Course Team" approach adopted at Open University, UK, for example, has been a very well known and tried out approach for the development of study materials of a high academic quality. In the Course Team approach "by working together as a team of group of academics, BBC producers, educational technologists, editors, designers, and others develop an integrated multimedia course. Producing course materials is primarily a corporate, not individual activity" (Sewart, 1989). A significant but different system is the one followed at the Fern University in Germany, where the sole responsibility of course material writing rests on the individual teacher, but in case he desires to incorporate media into his course materials, there is a separate unit to help him. This unit called the "Centre for the Development of Distance Education" has educational technologists and media experts and is equipped with modern media technologies. As and when the individual teacher writing the course requires, this centre not only helps in the incorporation of media but also undertakes the pedagogical evaluation and final production of the course materials.

While OU follows Course Team approach of UKOU, DEI to some extent follows German model in which individual teacher is given the sole responsibility of writing study materials devoid of media mix. Perhaps some thing like German Centre for the Development of Distance Education can be established either at the institutional level or at national level as a national resource centre for the development of study materials for distance education. The Director and Coordinator were asked a question as to who develops the study materials? In both the institutes, their internal staff is involved in the preparation of study materials with the help of outside experts. However, the staff strength (core faculty) in DEI is very less, just three only while OU is having nearly 300 core faculty. It is very strange that neither of the institutes uses study materials developed by other Distance Education Institutes or Open University. However, OUs study materials are used by some other Open Universities and Distance Education Institutes other than the institute under study.

TABLE 4.1

Involvement of People in Preparation of Study Material

Who develops the study materials?	*OU*	*DEI*
(a) Core faculty (internal)	—	—
(b) Outside experts	—	—
(c) Both staff and outside expert	Yes	Yes
(d) Use the material of other institute	No	No

Outside Experts

As we have seen the study materials are prepared by the core faculty as well as outside experts by both OU and DEI. In this section, an attempt has been made to study as to who are hired as experts and what procedures are adopted for asking them to write course materials. In case of DEI outside experts are subject specialists only. They are drawn from a panel of course writers prepared by DEI consisting of senior teachers of the constituent colleges teaching that particular subject as recommended by the principal of the college. There is no involvement of any media experts or educational technologists or even language editor. However, in OU people hired are both specialist in the subject as well as media experts. While OU hires people from all over the country, DEI gets its expertise mostly from its constituent colleges.

TABLE 4.2
Involvement of Experts in Study Material

People hired to write study materials are	*OU*	*DEI*
(a) Subject Specialist	—	Yes
(b) Media Experts	—	—
(c) Both (Specialist and Media Expert)	Yes	—
(d) Experienced Distance Educators	—	—

The procedures adopted for asking these experts to write the study materials were enquired through a question which is presented in Table 4.3 below. In DEI the experts are only sent a copy of the syllabus and asked to write the study materials. Occasionally a meeting of the course writer is organized to brief them about writing in a prescribed format. In OU a more structured outline is prepared for course development which include identifying media components, integrating media components, finalizing unit-wise course outlines and deciding themes for audio-video programmes.

TABLE 4.3
Procedure for writing Study Materials

Procedure for asking outside experts to write the study materials	*OU*	*DEI*
(a) They are sent syllabus and asked to write	—	Yes
(b) A guide book/instruction manual is sent	Yes	—
(c) They are called and instructions and training is given how to write study materials for Distance Education	Sometime	Sometimes

A minimum number of 4 to 5 experts are involved in writing course for OU while the minimum is only one, i.e. subject specialist in DEI. Very few teachers associated with writing course materials of DEI have received training/orientation programme in writing through SIM format.

Production of Study Material

The production of study materials involved the mechanical reproduction of the prepared study materials in presentable format. Presentable format implies the logical sequencing of content, provision of self-checking, exercises objectives and style (typography) of presentation.

Depending upon the objectives, learning content and the psycho educational background of the learners, different formats have been used to produce the course reading materials in distance education. In using different formats, it is usually assumed that the layout and general typography of a printed course may exert influence on its teaching effectiveness. Logical division of the text into reasonably short paragraphs and generous spacing of chapters, sections, and paragraphs can evidently help the students considerably. A number of headlines and sub-heads with appropriate use of italics or bold type to single out key concepts has been advocated.

The responses to a question pertaining to the use of prescribed format for printing study materials revealed that both the Institutes have a prescribed format for printing of the study materials. However, there is no graphics on the cover page study materials of DEI while it does have a variety of graphics in study material prepared by OU. Both the institutes have printing press of their own as also they hire the services of approved printers from outside.

TABLE 4.4

Use of Prescribed Format and Owning a Printing Press

		OU	*DEI*
(1)	Do you have a prescribed format for printing study materials ?	Yes	Yes
(2)	Do you have a printing press to print your own course materials ?	Yes	Yes

The DEI recognizes the importance of presenting the study materials in self-learning, it was realized by the researcher during the discussion that format having adequate figures and graphical presentations and the use of suitable typography but lack of adequate faculty, trained media personnel, educational technologist were reported as the main obstacles.

Evaluation of Study Materials

The term "evaluation" denotes different things in different contexts. Sometimes it refers to the assessment of students' performance to award grades/marks for various purposes; sometimes to the judgement of the complete educational system or components of it. This section is devoted to the evaluation of distance study materials. According to Holmberg (1985) this type of evaluation includes various attempts to obtain a good grasp of how courses function, how effective they are and how they are received by students and others' concerned. Summative evaluation is not what the distance educators are usually primarily interested in. However, they usually want to investigate courses with a view to improving them. This is known as formative evaluation which does not aim at passing judgement, but is to be seen as a component of the development work. The findings of the evaluation are meant to influence, modify or radically change the course presentation and study procedures.

In the light of the above, seeing formative evaluation as a component of development work for improving course materials, few items were included in the questionnaire to enquire about the practices/systems adopted for the evaluation of course materials. The results are presented in the following sections.

TABLE 4.5

Evaluation of Study Materials for Judging the Didactic Suitability

	OU	*DEI*
Are the study materials subject to evaluation for judging the didactic suitability for distance education students ?	Yes	No

Results indicate that DEI does not subject their study materials to any evaluation, where as it is being done by OU which aspects of study materials are subjected to evaluation are presented in Table 4.6 below.

TABLE 4.6

Aspects of Study Material Evaluated

	OU	DEI
Evaluation of course materials with		
(a) Relevance of content to course objectives	Yes	—
(b) Media aspects in study materials	—	—
(c) Style of presentation of the content	—	—
(d) Language difficulty	—	—

It has been reported by OU that evaluation was concerned with judging the relevance of the content of the reading materials to the objectives intended to be achieved.

How and by whom are these aspects of the study materials evaluated? People involved in evaluation of OU's study material include subject experts of the university and the course team including media experts and also the outside experts.

The Director and Coordinator were asked if students were involved in the process of evaluation with the intention of receiving feedback from them. The practice is neither being followed at OU nor at DEI.

TABLE 4.7

Intention Behind Students' Involvement

Are students involved in the process of evaluation with the intention of receiving feedback regarding	*OU*	*DEI*
(a) Quality of materials ?	No	No
(b) Language difficulty ?	No	No
(c) Comprehension ?	No	No

With respect to the process adopted for the evaluation of study materials, the response is given in the table.

TABLE 4.8
Process of Evaluation

The didactic suitability of the study materials is exactly judged by evaluating the	*OU*	*DEI*
(a) Process of judgement using wisdom	—	—
(b) Inviting criticism of experts in the field	Yes	—
(c) Through mutual discussion with colleagues	—	–
(d) By following standard guidelines	Yes	—

It is reported that criticism of experts in the field are invited to improve the study materials in OU as well as following standard guidelines for preparing course study materials.

Dispatch of Study Materials

A distance teaching institute necessarily requires an efficient organization for the distribution of study materials whereas such an organisation is not needed in the conventional university. In fact dispatching study materials appear to be a quite simple task; but in reality it is quite difficult and complicated. Due to large enrolment of students, the institute adopts a uniform policy with reasonable pacing, instead of dispatching learning materials according to individual students study pace. In this section, the dispatch policies of the DEI as well as OU have been surveyed.

TABLE 4.9
Dispatch Policy of Study Material

How are study materials dispatched to students?	*OU*	*DEI*
(a) In one lot (at the time of admission/during PCP)	No	Yes
(b) At regular intervals in lots	Yes	No
(c) When demanded by students	No	No
(d) After assignments of previous materials have been submitted	No	No

Results of the dispatch policy as given in above Table 4.9

indicated that at OU study materials are dispatched at regular intervals in lots to the students residential addresses, whereas at DEI the students collect the study materials personally from the institute at the time of admission in one lot provided all the books are available. Otherwise students are to collect the study materials at a later date.

Data pertaining to nature of the time interval, i.e. pacing indicates that, there is fixed time interval of three to four weeks during which time OU sends its study materials to the students. This is not applicable to the students of DEI as they collect the study materials during the time of admission.

TABLE 4.10
Nature and Length of Pacing

		OU	*DEI*
1.	What sort of pacing is introduced in dispatching study materials ?		
	(a) there is a fixed time interval	Yes	—
	(b) no fixed time interval	—	—
	(c) time interval depends upon length of materials	—	—
	(d) time interval depends upon students demands	—	—
2.	In case of fixed time interval of pacing, what is the exact length of time in weeks? 3 to 4 weeks	Yes	—

With respect to the system adopted for the management of the dispatch work, it was found that OU has a full-fledged Material Production and Distribution of Division (MPDD) which takes care of distribution of study material whereas at DEI, the study material unit does it manually where record of distribution of study materials to each student is maintained.

4.2.2 Assignment

As the UGC guidelines (1985) emphasise, the purpose of getting the assignment response sheets should be to ensure that :

(a) the students has understood and absorbed the course units sent to him;

(b) he knows how to organise the material involved;
(c) he gets a prompt evaluatory feedback which enables him to improve continuously through the comments/ suggestions for revision etc., that he received, and
(d) that he studies continuously throughout the year.

Every student at the under-graduate level should be required to do at least a total of 20 home assignments in all the subjects put together before he qualifies for the examination to be held at the end of that particular academic year. It is also expected that the assignment response sheets would be properly framed.

It would be necessary to frame statutory regulations in all the universities offering correspondence courses in regard to the submission of assignment response sheets. The student response sheets should be properly evaluated and promptly returned to the students with corrections, remarks, grade and suggestions for improvement. It must be ensured that all assignment response sheets are so returned within a stipulated period and the system must be notified in advance so that students know what to expect.

The evaluation of assignment response sheets must be done very carefully and thoroughly. The teachers should give detailed comments on the students written work and explain the faults in unambiguous terms. It would motivate the students to send their response sheets regularly.

Assignments act as a feedback device to support the student in his endeavour to learn of his own. In this section, the systems adopted for the management of feedback through assignments have been studied and analysed.

Regarding the condition of compulsory or voluntary submission of assignments, it was indicated that in DEI the concept of introducing assignment response sheet is yet to take place, though they are actively considering to implement the same. On the other hand, submission of assignment is a prerequisite for any examination conducted by OU and therefore it is and should be compulsory as a part of the continuous evaluation of students' performance. The present analysis on assignment is restricted to OU only.

TABLE 4.11
Submission of Assignments

		OU	DEI
1.	Is the submission of assignments compulsory ?	Yes	No
2.	Should the submission of assignments be optional	Yes	Yes

Purpose Served by Assignment

It was indicated by OU that assignments mainly serve two functions: (i) assessment of learner's performance, and (ii) learner support through instructional comments. and suggestions. Since submission of assignment is essential, the marks awarded in the assignment are included in the term end examination, therefore, it acts as an encouragement to the students to submit the required number of assignments (two per course).

Comments on Assignments

We have already examined earlier that assignments are only corrected for the purpose of awarding marks or for determining the eligibility of students for appearing in the term end examination. In distance education, however, assignments serve still a more important function, i.e. providing feedback to the students by removing their difficulties, giving suggestion for further improvement, pointing out one's weaknesses and strengths, etc. Such comments by the tutors written in an individualized form have real educational value, as they enable the students to know their faults and rectify them. Thus, a two-way postal communication is established between the teacher and the student and this forms the backbone of a good distance education system. The researcher being an academic counsellor in one of the IGNOU's programme is engaged in giving comments on assignments which are both personal as well as academic.

In Indian context, individualized personal comments referring to students works and achievements are written only in 35.71 percent institutions as reported in a study by Rathore (Rathore, 1993) in OU, however, it has been indicated that assignments are assessed by the academic counsellors (part time staff from outside) and nature of comments received on assignments are individualized and refers to students' achievements. The finding of this study corroborates the earlier findings by Rathore, 1993.

TABLE 4.12
Nature of Comments on Assignments

		OU	*DEI*
1.	Individualised comments referring to students' achievement.	Yes	No
2.	Non-individualized model solutions	Yes	No

Assignment Submission Time

Time taken to respond to assignments as reported by the Corordinator of IGNOU study centre reveals that normally 3 months time is given for submission of assignment. However, few days delay here and there is considered accepted taking into view that students are working people and have other priority too. Regarding number of pages to be written for each assignment, it has been reported that it ranges between 6-10 pages. However, in most of the assignment questions, word limit of writing the assignment is mentioned and students have to write it accordingly.

TABLE 4.13
No. of Pages and Time for Assignment Submission

	OU
How much time is given for submission of assignments for ?	3 months
Number of pages to be written for each assignment	6 to 10 pages

4.2.3 Personal Contact Programme

The UGC guidelines emphasise that, the provision of personal contact programmes should be regarded as an essential feature of correspondence through lectures, tutorials, seminars and discussion. The personal contact programmes through intensive classroom instructions, individual guidance and counselling help in giving a proper orientation to the students, add to their motivation, encourage regular study habit and instill confidence in them.

A contact programme of 20 working days at the undergraduate level and at least two programmes of 15 working days each at the post-graduate level should be organized in different places wherever there is a reasonably good number of students. There should also be an orientation programme of two days for post-graduate students. The programme at the post graduate level should be compulsory for every student.

In this context, what actually goes on during PCP? What is the nature of participation in PCP? What are the objectives behind organizing PCP ? etc. are some of the questions about PCPs addressed to in this section.

Organisation of PCP

In principle, as per the UGC guidelines, a PCP is required to be held at places wherever there is a concentration of more than 200 students. But in a city like Mumbai where large number of students enroll for distance education programmes, it becomes difficult to stick to it for reasons like, unavailability of an institution willing to host the programme, lack of accommodation for students in a particular area where there is high concentration of students' population, etc.

Duration, Frequency and Nature of PCP

As regards the frequency of PCPs, OU organizes PCP twice in a year for a period of at least 3 months each during March to May and September to November. It is being organized only on Sundays and a minimum of six lectures (15 hours) are organised per course. PCPs are organised in the beginning and towards the end of the course, and the nature of participation in PCP is optional/voluntary.

In DEI PCP's are organised for a period of 3 months in a year during January to March. PCP lectures are held during evening hours from 6.00 p.m. to 8.00 p.m. daily in the constituent colleges. PCP's are organized towards end of the course before examination. Like OU, six to seven lectures are organised per course in DEI. Participation in PCP's is voluntary.

However, there is a large turn out of students in the constituent colleges in which PCP is organized by IDE. Many times the number of students attending a PCP centre goes beyond 200, as a result of which it becomes difficult to accommodate all of them. Since large number of students turn up for participating in PCP, it implies that students need guidance and lectures. It is therefore not possible to give counselling to the students on an individual basis but to address the students through formal classroom teaching in a face to face manner. Lecture method is normally being used. Therefore, there is a need to have more PCP centres.

Table 4.14
Duration, Frequency and Nature of PCP

	OU	*DEI*
Duration of PCPs organised and frequency	(i) 6 months in a year (ii) only on Sundays (iii) 6 lectures per course (iv) In the beginning and towards the end of the year	(i) 3 months in a year (ii) Every day except Sundays (iii) 6 to 7 lectures per course (iv) At the end of the course but before exam.
Natue of participation in PCP	Voluntary	Voluntary

Venue and Staff of PCP

In OU, Personal Contact Programmes are organised in their three Study Centres located in Mumbai and the staffs engaged in PCP are the academic counsellors (part time) drawn from the local resources. In DEI, the PCPs are organised in the constituent colleges affiliated to the University of Mumbai and normally the faculty members of that particular college in which PCP is organised act as the resource persons in that centre.

Objectives behind PCPs

In order to study the objectives which the institutes had behind organizing PCP, for the students, a list of 9 possible aims were given to the Director and Coordinator (Table 4.15). They were asked to tickmark if the given objective was applicable in their case, and if applicable then they were further asked to rank them.

From the data it becomes clear that at OU, the first priority aim of organising the PCPs was to conduct session to remove learning difficulties followed by providing individual tutoring and counselling to students as second priority. The third priority was to use PCPs as a platform to organize seminars and group discussion and the fourth priority was to orient students with distance teaching and learning and disseminate other information.

At DEI, the first priority was to formally teach the contents to students followed by to prepare students for forthcoming final examination. The third priority was to conduct session to remove the learning difficulties and the forth one was to introduce the faculty and staff to the students.

From the findings, it appears that students of DEI as perceived by the Institute are more oriented towards completing their examination and getting a degree as most of them are freshers. Therefore, PCPs should be organised towards meeting that end.

TABLE 4.15
Objectives behind PCP—Priority Rank

Objectives behind organization of PCPs are :	*OU*	*DEI*
(i) To formally teach the content to students		1
(ii) To conduct session to remove the learning difficulties.	1	3
(iii) To provide individual tutoring and counselling to students.	2	
(iv) To prepare the students for the forthcoming final examination.		2
(v) To use PCPs as a platform to organize seminars and group discussion.	3	
(vi) To introduce the faculty and staff to the students.		4
(vii) To orient students with distance teaching and learning and disseminate other information.	4	
(viii) To encourage students to use the facilities at the study centre.		
(ix) To show audio/video cassettes during PCP.		

Purpose Served by PCPs

Though we will get a true picture at the purposes served by PCPs in this second part when we examine students' perceptions regarding them, as they are the real beneficiaries of these contact programmes. However, it is worth noting as to what purposes are perceived to be served during the PCPs by the Director/Coordinator.

From the analysis it is indicated that during PCP the study materials are supplemented by teaching. Thus the first aim to be achieved by IDE. Similarly, in IGNOU students academic problems are removed, therefore, the first aim of PCP as identified by IGNOU to be conduct sessions to remove the learning difficulties are achieved. The data given in the Table is self-explanatory.

TABLE 4.16

Purpose Served by PCPs : Priority Rank

	OU	*DEI*
Which of the following purposes are served by PCPs at your institute ?		
(i) Learner isolation is removed		5
(ii) Study materials are supplemented by teaching		1
(iii) Students' academic problems are removed	1	3
(iv) Students' preparation for final examination is ensured		2
(v) Students are encouraged to put forward their academic and personal problem.	2	4
(vi) Support with the faculty of distance teaching system is established		
(vii) Students are encouraged to make better effective use of facilities at the study centre.	4	
(viii) Students' learning and academic achievement is increased	3	

4.2.4 Study Centre

The UGC guidelines further emphasises that, high priority should be given to the setting up of study centres outside the headquarters in areas where there is a reasonable concentration of students. There should be a study centre for every group of

500 students in an area. Each Study Centre should not only have adequate library facilities (text books, and reference materials) but also have part-time instruction, counselling so as to advise the student on the course material and on the individual difficulties of students. Advantage should be taken of the existing physical facilities and part time staff in the colleges for running these centres.

The centres could be developed for listening to radio talks and tape lectures of audio and video cassettes.

Normally a study centre should be equipped with (a) a small library, (b) audio-video cassettes, (c) a computer terminal, (d) adequate facilities for sitting, reading and writing work, and (e) staffed by a team of part time counsellors. With this picture and functions of study centres in mind, the Director and Co-ordinator were asked questions relating to the study centre support systems which are presented below.

TABLE 4.17

Institutions offering Study Centre Facilities

	OU	*DEI*
Does your institute has study centres of its own ?	Yes	No

It was found that although OU has three study centres in Mumbai, the DEI has no study centres of its own as per the concept and functions of a study centre is outlined here as per the guidelines of UGC.

However, the DEI has PCP centres wherein face to face teaching and annual examinations for DEI students are conducted. PCP centres are therefore called examination centres in DEI. As outlined what a study centre should be equipped with, the PCP centres of DEI does not fit into the category of being labeled as a study centre.

The implication of this finding is that, when UGC and DEC has made it a requirement for the distance education institutes to have the provision of study centres the DEI must think seriously of introducing the concept of study centres for better Student Support Services.

Facilities Extended

An enquiry about the facilities extended at the study centres was made which had three parts pertaining to library facilities, media facilities and tutoring/counselling services. The results pertaining to library facilities reveal that only OU offers library facilities at their study centres. In these libraries text books, study materials, reference books and journals and periodicals are provided to the students.

TABLE 4.18
Library Facilities at Study Centre

	OU	*DEI*
Does your Institute extend Library facility at study centres ?	Yes	No
If yes, does it include :		
Study materials	Yes	—
Text books	Yes	—
Reference books	Yes	—
Journals and periodicals	Yes	—

With regard to media facilities extended in the study centres, the results indicated that only OU extends media facilities at their study centres. It is interesting to note that all

TABLE 4.19
Media Facilities

	OU	*DEI*
Does your Institūte extend media facility at the study centres ?	Yes	No
If yes, does it include :		
Aduio tapes	Yes	—
Video tapes	Yes	—
Television	Yes	—
Computer	Yes	—
Films	Yes	—
Radio	Yes	—

the media facilities including audio tapes, video tapes, television, computer, films and radio are provided in the study centres to the students on demand.

As far as tutoring/counselling services offered at the study centres are concerned, it was found that once again only OU offers these services. The details pertain to this is given in Table 4.19 which is self-explanatory.

TABLE 4.20
Tutoring/Counselling Services

	OU	*DEI*
Does your Institute offer tutoring/counselling services at the study centres ?	Yes	No
If yes, does it include :		
(i) Is there only one tutor/counsellor for all subjects?	No	—
(ii) Are there many for different subjects?	Yes	—
(iii) Are they full time employees ?	No	—
(iv) Are they part time employees ?	Yes	—
(v) Are they available every day ?	Yes	—

Functions of Study Centres

As already mentioned earlier, the study centres serve definite support functions in distance education. In the context four functions have been identified which are provided by OU. This finding is presented in Table 4.21

TABLE 4.21
Functions of Study Centres

	OU	*DEI*
What are the functions of your study centres ?		
(i) Sale and acceptance of admission forms	Yes (only sale)	No
(ii) Organising face to face teaching	Yes	Yes
(iii) Counselling on academic and administrative matters	Yes	No
(iv) Support of distance learning through the use of A.V. aids	Yes	No

It has been reported by the Coordinator of OU study centre that there are nearly 1600 students attached to their study centre. According to OU norms there should be a study centre for every 500 students. But the study centres having more than 500 students should have additional appointment of Assistant coordinators for the purpose. It has also been observed that 25 to 50 percent of the students attached to study centres make use of the facilities provided to them as presented in Table 4.22.

TABLE 4.22
Attendance at the Study Centre

	OU	DEI
(1) How many students attached to a study centre make use of the facilities provided to them ?	25-50 percent	—
(2) How many students are attached to one study centre ?	1600 Students	—-

Utilisation of Facilities

With regard to the individual utilization of each facility offered at the study centre, it was found that tutoring and counselling was utilized by 40 percent students followed by face to face teaching by 30 percent students. While library facility was being used by 10 percent students, all other facilities were

TABLE 4.23
Utilisation of Individual Facilities

Please indicate from the list below the utilization of each facility by the students by approximate % of its use	*OU*	*DEI*
(1) Library facility	10	—
(2) Tutoring & counselling	40	—
(3) Audio Tapes	5	—
(4) Video Tapes	5	—
(5) Films	5	—
(6) Computer	5	—
(7) Face to face teaching	30	—

being used by 5 percent of the students as reported by the coordinator.

4.2.5 Other Support System

We have discussed and examined earlier the major support systems adopted by distance education institutes to supplement distance teaching and support independent learning. We have examined the four components of Student Support Services namely, Study Materials, Assignments, Personal Contact Progamme and Study Centre support systems. However, pre-enrolment guidance/counselling and measures taken for reducing dropout rates are two very important services that have been left out. In this section, a stock of these additional support systems, if any adopted by the institutes has been taken.

Pre-enrolment Guidance/Counselling Service

Pre-enrolment guidance/Counselling means providing of information about methods, procedures, materials and requirements of distance education to all those prospective learners who desire to take admission into distance education courses. Distance study is a special kind of study approach requiring hard work like responding to submission of assignments, participating in personal contact programme, lectures, library/self-study work, etc. Many people join distance study courses without properly understanding these requirements only to later realize that they cannot cope up with them and dropout. Distance Education Institutes, cautious of success and dropout rates of students arrange to provide pre-enrolment guidance/counselling to all those prospective students who approach them with such queries.

In the distance teaching universities of developed countries, like the UK Open University, and the Fern University, Germany, Pre-enrolment guidance is provided to the students almost as a regular feature. Results of studies (Bartels, 1982) conducted on this aspect in these countries have shown to increase the success rates and decrease the dropout rates.

It is in this context, an attempt has been made in this section to study if such a pre-enrolment guidance/counselling is provided to the prospective students or not and the measures taken for dropouts.

In order to study the details of the pre-enrolment guidance/counselling provided, if any, a question was designed for the Director and coordinator to collect relevant information from the institutes. The responses given by the institutions is presented in Table 4.24.

TABLE 4.24
Details of Pre-enrolment Guidance/Counselling

	OU	*DEI*
Does your institute offer pre-enrolment guidance/ counselling service to people who desire to undertake distance study with you ?		
If yes, does this include :	No	No
(a) Written correspondence with those who make queries		
(b) Face to face counselling with those who approach		
(c) Both the above (a) & (b)		
(1) In case of written correspondence, do you send :		
(a) Pre-produced non-individualised letter?		
(b) Individualised letters referring to specific queries?		
(2) In case of face to face counselling do you :		
(a) have a formal department/section and staff for this ?		
(b) do it on the demands of the students?		

Counselling to Check Non-Starter/Dropout Rates

The dropout rates are quite high in distance teaching universities all over the world. Thus, distance teaching universities adopt different systems of counselling their students who are non-starter or who drops out of the studies. A non-starter in distance education is a student who seeks enrolment but never gives an indication of beginning his studies, by way of responding to assignments or otherwise. On the other hand a dropout is one who begins his study but after sometime discontinues the studies for a variety of reason best known to him. It is in this context an attempt was made to study whether the distance education institutes are concerned about the non-starter and dropout rates?

TABLE 4.25

Counselling for Non-Starters/Dropouts

	OU	*DEI*
Does your institute contact students who discontinue their studies?	No	No
(1) The institute contacts the students and try to do counseling.	No	No
(2) The initiative is left to students.	Yes	Yes

It is observed that neither OU, nor DEI contacts the students who are either non-starter or who dropsout for counselling. However, the initiative is left to the students. Personal query with the Director/Coordinator revealed that it is very seldom that a student comes to discuss his problems. However, whenever they do come, they are given proper guidance and counselling. Thus it can be safely concluded that the distance education institutes are not at all concerned with the problem of non-starter and dropout rates in their system of distance education.

As regards the specific measures taken to check the non-starter and dropout rates, it was found that only OU sent pre-produced standard letters of encouragement or reminders to the students. No distance education institute sends letter written in personal style. OU also occasionally gives phone calls to students. Thus only postal counselling was the only measure taken to check this problem. How far is this postal counselling

TABLE 4.26

Measures Taken to Check Non-starter and Dropout Rates

	OU	*DEI*
What measures does your Institute take to reduce non-starter and dropout rates?		
(a) Mailing of pre-produced letters of encouragement/ reminders	Yes	No
(b) Mailing of individual letters	No	No
(c) Phone calls to students	Yes	No
(d) No efforts	No	Yes

effective for checking non-starter and dropout rates in distance education is an interesting area for further research ?

Other supporting systems which were discussed with the Director and the coordinator are given below.

Regarding continuous assessment of students performance for monitoring learners progress OU insists on compulsory submission of written assignments, whereas DEI does not ask for submission of assignments to its students. In OU term end examinations are conducted twice in a year, i.e. June and December. In DEI annual examinations are held in April/May and supplementary examinations in October/November. Students are given freedom to decide when they would like to sit in the final examination in both the institutes. While the validity period of admission to under graduate programmes of OU is 8 years, it is for a period of 5 years for the students of DEI. Therefore, students can attempt any number of examinations during these periods.

PART TWO

4.3 PERCEPTION OF STUDENTS REGARDING STUDENT SUPPORT SERVICES

This part critically examines the provision of Student Support Services from students' point of view and their perceptions about the facilities available to them. This section deals with the second objective and the research question of the study which are stated below.

Objective 2

'To critically study the provision of Student Support Services from students, point of view and the perception of the students'.

Research Question 2

What students feel about the quality and quantity of the services provided and the extent of their use ?

4.3.1 Study Materials (Students' Perception)

In distance education printed study materials expressly serve the individual learner in the study of his own. The quality and didactic suitability of the study materials for independent/self-learning not only enhances students' learning but also determines the academic credibility of distance education. The print media in the form of study materials dominates the other forms of technological mass communication media and constitutes the mainstay in distance education. Therefore, printed study materials form the backbone of any distance education programme. Even in advance countries of the world where open universities and highly developed mass communication media have brought about revolutionary changes in education methods, printed study materials is still the most important means of imparting instruction to thousands of learners at a distance.

As the students are the main users of the study materials their opinion as to what they think of the materials they study is of extreme importance. Nobody else than the students can tell whether the materials are suitable for their study which they are doing on their own. In fact, students attitudes towards the study materials have been taken as a criteria to judge the effectiveness of the study materials in a number of research studies. In this study too, students were asked what they think about the study materials generally, how interesting and lively it is etc. They were also asked specific questions with a view to improving study materials presentation and give suggestions for improvement. This part, thus, evaluates the study materials supplied by DEI and OU in the light of feedback received from the students.

The students were asked to respond to question number 1 to 8 in which qualities, considered essential for an effective distance teaching study materials, were presented. They were asked to mark yes or no if the quality in question was present in the study materials supplied to them. The response of the students is presented in Table 4.27 which is nevertheless self-explanatory.

The overall percentages in Table 4.27 reveals that on the whole almost every student (more than 70 percent) finds all the qualities present in the supplied study materials except the

TABLE 4.27

Qualities present in the Study Materials

		Yes		No		Total
		f	%	f	%	
Q.1. Do you find the supplied study materials different from Text book in its format and persentation?	OU	40	(71.4)	16	(28.6)	56
	DEI	70	(70.0)	30	(30.0)	100
	Total	110	(70.5)	46	(29.5)	156
Q.2. Do you find the presentation and type setting of study materials interesting and effective?	OU	48	(85.7)	08	(14.3)	56
	DEI	64	(62.7)	38	(37.3)	102
	Total	112	(70.9)	46	(29.1)	158
Q.3. While reading the supplied study materials, do you feel as if your teacher is communicating with you?	OU	40	(74.1)	14	(25.9)	54
	DEI	37	(37.0)	63	(63.0)	100
	Total	77	(50.0)	77	(50.0)	154
Q.4. Do the study materials enable you to understand the concepts intended to be taught?	OU	48	(85.7)	08	(14.3)	56
	DEI	70	(70.0)	30	(30.0)	100
	Total	118	(75.6)	38	(24.4)	156
Q.5. Do you find the study materials interesting and lively?	OU	52	(96.3)	02	(3.7)	54
	DEI	66	(66.0)	34	(34.0)	100
	Total	118	(76.6)	36	(23.4)	154
Q.6. Do the self-checking exercises at the end of each unit serve your purpose?	OU	48	(85.7)	08	(14.3)	56
	DEI	73	(73.0)	27	(27.0)	100
	Total	121	(77.6)	35	(22.4)	156
Q.7. Do you find the language of the supplied study materials easy to comprehend?	OU	52	(92.9)	04	(7.1)	56
	DEI	72	(72.0)	28	(28.0)	100
	Total	124	(79.5)	32	(20.5)	156
Q.8. Do the study materials contain enough illustrations, figure and diagrams to explain the concepts?	OU	34	(60.7)	22	(39.3)	56
	DEI	58	(58.0)	42	(42.0)	100
	Total	92	(59.0)	64	(41.0)	156

question number 3 and 8 which deals with effecting didactic communication through study materials (mainly self-instructional format) and the presence of enough illustrations, figures and diagrams in the study materials. While 74.1 percent of OU students feel that the study material involves two-way communication, 63 percent of the students of DEI do not feel that the study material is written in a way which involves two way communication.

Whether the study materials contain enough illustrations, figures and diagrams to explain the concept to this question 60.7 percent of OU students and 58 percent of DEI students affirms that the study materials contain enough illustrations, figures and diagrams. It is therefore, revealed that the supplied study materials donot possess the above two qualities (not ùpto mark) which needs to be taken care.

Reading Habits of the Students

Question number 9, 10, 11 and 12 in the questionnaire for students were designed to assess the reading habits of the students and the number of pages they are expected to read every day. The first two questions were asked to give the number of units read and the number of pages expected to be read each day respectively. The variations in the response, of 103 students who gave responses to these questions was so great that practically it was difficult to tabulate them. However, it was indicated that 52.4 percent students have read 1-10 pages, 24.3 percent have read 11-20 pages, 13.6 percent have read 21-30 pages and 09.7 percent have read more than 31 pages each day. There is though not much variations among the students of OU & DEI, more than 50 percent of the students read about 1 to 10 pages each day.

TABLE 4.28

Number of Pages Expected to be Read Per Day

Range of pages	*OU*		*DEI*		*Total*	
	f	*%*	*f*	*%*		
1-10	20	(52.6)	34	(52.3)	54	(53.4)
11-20	06	(15.8)	19	(29.2)	25	(24.3)
21-30	10	(26.3)	04	(06.2)	14	(13.6)
31 and above	02	(05.3)	08	(12.3)	10	(09.7)
Total	38		65		103	

On the whole it appears that the institutions do not put much reading workload on their students. How do students perceive this workload was the concern of question number 11 and 12. The data in Table 4.29 indicates that a majority of 74.4 percent students do not find that their institutions put too much workload on them. Only 25.6 percent students think that their institutions put too much reading workload on them.

TABLE 4.29
Institutional Workload

		Yes		No		Total
		f	%	f	%	
Do you think that your institution puts too much reading/workload on its students?	OU	16	(28.6)	40	(71.4)	56
	DEI	24	(24.0)	76	(76.0)	100
	Total	40	(25.6)	116	(74.4)	156

Despatch of Study Materials

The question number 19 in the students' questionnaire pertains to the mode of despatch of study materials to the students. It was revealed from Table 4.30 that while in OU 66.7 percent of the students received their study materials by Registered Post, it is only 6.7 percent in DEI. On the other hand while 91.1 percent students of DEI received their study materials by hand delivery it was only 3.7 percent students in OU.

TABLE 4.30
Mode of Sending Study Material

How is the study material sent?	*Regd. Post*		*Ordinary Post*		*Hand Delivery*		*Total*
	f	%	f	%	f	%	
OU	36	(66.7)	16	(29.6)	02	(3.7)	54
DEI	06	(6.7)	02	(2.2)	82	(91.1)	90
Total	42	(29.2)	18	(12.5)	84	(58.3)	144

By and large OU sends its study materials by registered post whereas DEI students collect their study materials from the counters of DEI building. However, it has also been reported that 29.6 percent of the students of OU receive their study materials by ordinary post. Now, whether the study materials are sent in one lot is being examined in question number 17 which is given.

TABLE 4.31
Volume on Study Materials

	Are the study materials sent in one lot?				
	Yes		*No*		
	f	*%*	*f*	*%*	*Total*
OU	40	(71.4)	16	(28.6)	56
DEI	43	(43.0)	57	(57.0)	100
Total	83	(53.2)	73	(46.8)	156

It is observed that majority of the students of OU, i.e. 71.4 percent receive their study materials in one lot while less than 50 percent of the students of DEI receive their study materials in one lot. It may be due to the fact study materials of DEI may not be available for distribution amongst the students on the date of admission as a result of which students are told to receive their study materials at a later date. This has a very serious implication as the DEI must plan their requirement of study materials well in advance.

Further a question was asked whether you are satisfied with the quantity of study materials sent?

TABLE 4.32
Satisfaction Regarding Quantity of Study Material

	Are you satisfied with the quantity of study materials sent?				
	Yes		*No*		
	f	*%*	*f*	*%*	*Total*
OU	44	(81.5)	10	(18.5)	54
DEI	66	(66.0)	34	(34.0)	100
Total	110	(71.4)	44	(28.6)	154

It is observed that while 81.5 percent of the students of OU are satisfied with the quantity of study materials sent, 34.0 percent of DEI students are not satisfied with the quantity of study materials sent. As we have seen earlier, DEI students do not receive their study materials in one lot but in bits and pieces, hence the dissatisfaction.

Improvements Wanted

The question number 20 was designed to elicit from students the suggestion, which they would like to be incorporated for improving the despatch system. The results of this are presented in Table 4.33 which are self-revealing.

It is clearly noted that the first priority improvement would be to send the materials, only after the assignments for the previous materials have been submitted and checked. It is further clear that quantity of materials sent is not a bothering factor, but quantity of study materials sent should not be reduced.

TABLE 4.33

Priority for Improvements in Despatch System

Which of the following improvements would you like to have in the distribution system?		*Yes*		*No*		*Total*
		f	*%*	*f*	*%*	
(a) Quantity of Study materials sent be reduced	OU	16	(33.3)	32	(66.7)	48
	DEI	27	(30.3)	62	(69.7)	89
	Total	43	(31.4)	94	(68.6)	137
(b) Students should be given freedom to decide both quantity and quality	OU	18	(39.1)	28	(60.9)	46
	DEI	55	(60.4)	36	(39.6)	91
	Total	73	(53.3)	64	(46.7)	137
(c) Quantity is Ok but pacing should be decided by students	OU	16	(40.0)	24	(60.0)	40
	DEI	37	(43.5)	48	(56.5)	85
	Total	53	(42.4)	72	(57.6)	125
(d) Materials be sent only after the assignments for the previous materials have been submitted and checked	OU	18	(40.9)	26	(59.1)	44
	DEI	51	(60.0)	34	(40.0)	85
	Total	69	(53.5)	60	(46.5)	129

TABLE 4.34
Satisfaction with Study Materials

	On the whole, are you satisfied with the supplied study materials?				*Total*
	Yes		*No*		
	f	*%*	*f*	*%*	
OU	50	(92.6)	04	(7.4)	54
DEI	67	(67.0)	33	(33.0)	100
Total	117	(76.0)	37	(24.0)	154

It is seen that 76 percent students are on the whole satisfied with the study materials, leaving only 24 percent students who have some complains about the study material. However across the universities, while 92 percent of OU students are satisfied with the supplied study materials, only 67 percent of DEI students are satisfied. It is seen that 33 percent students of DEI are not satisfied with the study materials implying that the study materials are not upto the mark and hence needs immediate attention of the authority.

Further, in response to the call to give open suggestions for improving the quality of study materials, the following observations of the students are worth consideration :

(i) Previous question papers should be appended to the study materials so that it helps the students in preparing for the examination better.

(ii) Study materials should have colour diagrams, charts, contemporary examples and list of reference books.

(iii) Study materials should be in other languages too. At present it is only in English in OU and English and Marathi (only in selected subjects) in DEI.

(iv) It has been suggested by the students of DEI that the study materials be prepared in easy and simple languages and be devoid of spelling mistakes.

(v) Self-check exercises and more questions to be added in the study material.

(vi) Students of DEI suggested that study materials should be available in all the subjects.

(vii) Students of OU have suggested that latest developments and case studies should be included instead of reprint of old version.

(viii) Students of both the institutes have suggested that the study materials be of question answer type.

(ix) Shortage of study materials should be taken care and adequate number of study materials be printed before the admission process starts.

4.3.2 Assignments (Students' Perception)

Two-way communications occurs between the student and the teacher in the supporting distance teaching institutes : the real communication in writing through assignment, on the telephone, by computer or face to face contact and simulated communication that can be, and often is, brought about by style of presentation of the study materials. The Response Sheet Assignments are widely used as a device for non-contiguous two-way communication, between the student and teacher to serve the following purposes in distance education. (Hoimberg, 1985):

(a) to support students' motivation and interest by contact with an encouraging tutor or counsellor;

(b) to support and facilitate student learning by having students apply the knowledge and skills acquired as well as by tutor's comments, explanations and suggestions; and

(c) To assess students' progress in order to provide them with an instrument by means of which they can judge their educational situation and needs and by means of which marks can be awarded.

In practice the assignments act as a feed back device to support the student in his endeavor to learn of his own. The feedback comes in the form of constructive explanation, comments and suggestions from the teacher evaluating the assignment response sheets submitted by the students. In case the student hás some doubts or problems, still after receiving the tutor's comments, he writes back to the tutor who replies the queries and removes doubts in writing. In this way, a two-way communication through written media is established between the student and the teacher.

In this section, since the DEI has not yet introduced the concept of submission of assignments by its students as a part of continuous evaluation of the performance of the students, only the response of the students of OU has been analysed here.

TABLE 4.35
Requirement of Assignment Submission

	Are you required to submit assignments ?				Total
	Yes		No		
	f	%	f	%	
OU	52	(92.9)	04	(2.6)	56
DEI	00	(0.0)	120	(100)	120

Table 4.35 reveals that submission of assignments is a requirement in OU while it is not so in DEI.

TABLE 4.36
Purposes Served by Assignments

Is the main purpose of assignment, assessment or feedback or both?	*OU*	
	f	*(%)*
1. Assessment	08	(14.8)
2. Feedback	04	(7.4)
3. Both Assessment and feedback	42	(77.8)
Total	54	

The results in Table 4.36 indicate that assignments serve the exclusive function of assessment of students' performance only for 14.8 percent students and as feedback in 7.4 percent students. However, for 77.8 percent students, assignments serve both the purpose of assessment as well as feedback. Hence, assignments serve both the examination function and giving feedback to the students for improving.

Regarding the number of assignments submitted by the students, the data presented in Table 4.37 revealed that 23.1

TABLE 4.37
Number of Assignments

How many assignments do you submit in each paper?	OU	
	f	%
Two assignments	12	(23.1)
Three assignments	38	(73.1)
Six assignments	02	(3.8)
Total	52	

percent students submitted two assignments in each paper while 73.1 percent students submitted three assignments in each paper. It is therefore, very clear that submission of 2 to 3 assignments in each paper is required for determining eligibility to sit for the term end examination in OU.

TABLE 4.38
Submission Time of Assignment

How much time is taken for submission of assignment responses?	OU Number of Respondents				
	One Month	Two Months	Three Months	Four Months	Total
	08 (16.7)	20 (41.7)	16 (33.3)	04 (8.4)	48

Time taken to respond to average assignments also varied across the sample of students. Data in Table 4.38 indicates that nearly 16.7 percent students took one month time for submission of assignments, whereas 41.7 percent students took two months for submission of assignments. However, only 33.3 percent took three months for submission of assignments. Normally, within a month's time assignments are to be submitted. It appears students take their own time in submitting the assignments and the management at study centre should take precautionary measure in this regard.

As far as student's desires, regarding the length of work required and time taken to respond to the assignments, are

TABLE 4.39
Student's Desire about Length and Responding Time of Assignments

Would you like the length of the assignment and time taken to respond to them to be :	*OU*	
	f	%
(1) Reduced	14	(25.9)
(2) Increased	10	(18.5)
(3) The same	30	(55.6)
Total	54	

concerned a majority of 55.6 percent students expressed the desire that the length of the assignments and time taken to respond to them should remain the same (Table 4.39).

However, 25.9 percent students expressed the desire to reduce the length of assignments and time taken to respond to them; whereas 18.5 percent student desired that both be increased.

On the basis of the results it can be safely concluded that students on the whole view the submission of assignments positively as it is indicated by more number of students. Further the quantum work required to be done to respond to give assignments is also not bothering as 18.5 percent students want that the length of assignments and the time taken to respond to them should be increased. This finding has important implications for distance education system. For example, our system can, in fact should rely more on non-contiguous two-way communication through assignments than personal contact/face to face communication. This is not only cost effective but also in line with the philosophy of distance education.

Turn Around Time

The time gap, from the day a student sends/posts his response sheets pertaining to the assignments to the day he receives them back duly marked and commented from his institution is called "Turn-around time". This time gap is particularly very important in distance education as it determines the quality and the value of feedback provided to the student through assignments. The longer is the turn around time, the delayed is the feedback, and we know that too much delayed feedback may loose its very purpose. Hence to ensure timely feedback through tutor comments on assignments, distance education system adopts management strategies that reduce turn around time. It is generally agreed that a turn around time of two to three weeks is quite a satisfactory time gap; which any effective distance teaching organization must strive to achieve.

In the Indian context students reported a turn around time of minimum 15 days to a maximum of 90 days, with more than 50 percent students reporting it between 30 to 50 days. Earlier in this study, it is reported that nearly 58 percent students took between 1 to 2 months for submission of assignments.

These students were further asked a question (Q. 26) Is the present turn around time suitable for your studies? The response indicated that for 67.9 percent students the present turn around time was suitable (Table 4.40), but for 32.1 percent students, the present turn around time was not suitable. Hence, it is desired that the distance education institute must adopt management systems to stick to assignments turn around time to the desired time lag of 15 to 21 days.

TABLE 4.40
Suitability of present Turn around time

	OU				
	Yes		*No*		*Total*
	f	*%*	*f*	*%*	
Is the present turnaround time suitable for your studies?	38	(67.9)	18	(32.1)	56

Usefulness of Assignments

The students were asked a question; Are the assignments useful to you? In response to this question 85.7 percent students replied that assignments are useful to them. Further they were cross-examined by asking them. 'Does the assignment as a whole test the main things the students need. In response it was found that 67.9 percent students responded positively while only 32.1 percent students replied in negative. It is thus evident that, whatever the purpose of assignments be perceived by the students : be it for the purpose of feedback or for examination purpose, it is useful to majority of the students.

TABLE 4.41
Usefulness of Assignment

	OU				
	Yes		*No*		*Total*
	f	%	*f*	%	
Are the assignments useful to you?	48	(85.7)	08	(14.3)	56
Do the assignments as a whole test the main things the students needs?	38	(67.9)	18	(32.1)	56

Value of Comments on Assignments

In this section, an attempt has been made to judge the value of the supplied comments and model solutions from the students point of view, i.e., what they actually receive, how they value it for their study; and are they satisfied in general with the assignments system.

In cases where teachers, besides checking, also give their comments on the assignments, it was found that:

(a) 76.0 percent students were satisfied with the teachers' comments and 24.0 percent were not satisfied (refer Table 4.42);
(b) In the case of 68.0 percent students' comments were personally written pointing out their individual mistakes but they were not written in this style for 32.0 percent students;
(c) In the opinion of 48.0 percent students the comments written were too general to make much sense for improvement but this was not the case for 52.0 percent students;
(d) In the opinion of 52.0 percent students, however, the

comments were quite comprehensive to let them understand their weakness, but such was not the opinion of 48.0 percent students;

(e) The comments motivated and helped in improving learning of 54.2 percent students, but in the case of 45.8 percent students they did not do this;

(f) The comments motivated 69.6 percent students to consult further study materials/journals/reference books etc., but they did not motivate 30.4 percent students; and finally;

(g) Only in the opinion of 37.5 percent students, the comments were just written in formality and did not prove to be of any use to them, but 62.5 percent students were opposed to this opinion.

From this data it appears as if the comments are doing the right job, because more than 75 percent students are satisfied;

TABLE 4.42

Students Reactions to Comments Received

If the teacher, besides checking, also sends their comments upon the assignment, then:	*OU*				
	Yes		*No*		*Total*
	f	*%*	*f*	*%*	
(A) Are you satisfied with these comments ?	38	(76.0)	12	(24.0)	50
(B) Are they personally written pointing out your individual mistakes?	34	(68.0)	16	(32.0)	50
(C) Are the comments too general to make much sense for your improvements?	24	(48.0)	26	(52.0)	50
(D) Are they comprehensive enough to let you understand your weakness?	26	(52.0)	24	(48.0)	50
(E) Do they motivate you and help you in improving your learning?	26	(54.2)	22	(45.8)	48
(F) Do they motivate you to consult further study materials/Journals/ reference books?	32	(69.6)	14	(30.4)	46
(G) Are the comments just written in a formality and don't prove to be useful to you?	18	(37.5)	30	(62.5)	48

perceive them to be of some use to them, and more than 50 percent students view them positively.

As regards the value of Model solutions/answers sent alongwith corrected assignments, the results obtained were quite surprising. Unexpectedly, the model solutions were perceived to help the process of learning by 85.7 percent students (Table 4.43), they helped 89.3 percent students in removing their doubts and mistakes; they motivate 85.7 percent students to do better; and they help 88.9 percent students in their preparations for final examination.

TABLE 4.43

Students' Reactions to Model Solutions Sent

If model answers are sent along with checked assignments, then do they help you in	*OU*				
	Yes		*No*		*Total*
	f	*%*	*f*	*%*	
(a) The process of learning	48	(85.7)	08	(14.3)	56
(b) Removing your doubts and mistakes	50	(89.3)	06	(10.7)	56
(c) Motivating to do better	48	(85.7)	08	(14.3)	56
(d) Preparing for examination	48	(88.9)	06	(11.1)	54

These findings are unexpected because model solutions or answers are not written in a two-way communication style. They actually lack, what Holmberg (1985) refers to as, two-way-didactic conversation between the tutor and the student. Hence, instead of serving as a tool to clarify the intricate relationships of difficult concepts and theories at higher levels of cognition, the model solutions often act as ready made guides and encourage students to memories than putting pressure on their mental faculties to process information at higher and more desirable levels of cognition. For these reasons the use of model solutions in general cannot be advocated in distance education except in the case of certain mathematical problems. Any way, as it is, the fact stands (as far as the findings of this study are valid) that model solutions have been perceived by the students (as it appears in face) to be more helpful than tutor comments. The only explanation for this, that comes to mind, is that probably the students value more the acquisition of degrees than the acquisition of knowledge. No doubt, it is an interesting area for further research; attempts should be made to study the comparative effectiveness of model solutions *vis-à-vis* tutor's comments in providing feedback to students; and at what costs?

Contribution of Assignment System

As regards the contribution of assignments, 92.9 percent students consider that submission of assignments help in general. More particularly 89.3 percent students consider that submission of assignments helps in the process of learning. Similarly, 92.9 percent of the students view that the submission of assignments helps them in their preparation for examinations (refer Table 4.44). These are highly encouraging findings which imply that the assignment system should be strengthened, both qualitatively and quantitatively.

TABLE 4.44
Contribution of Assignments

	OU				
	Yes		*No*		*Total*
	f	*%*	*f*	*%*	
Does the submission of assignments help you?	52	92.9)	04	(7.1)	56
(a) In the process of learning	50	(89.3)	06	(10.7)	56
(b) In your preparation for examination	52	(92.9)	04	(7.1)	56

Students' Satisfaction

The purpose of this question was to get an overall picture of the quality of assignments towards the learning of students and to see if the students were satisfied with it or not.

Pertaining to the students' satisfaction with quality of assignments, it was found (Table 4.45) that 85.2 percent students were satisfied with the overall quality of questions asked in the assignments. Further, 82.1 percent students were satisfied with quality of work they were expected to do to respond to the assignments.

The questions pertaining to Assignments in general (altogether 13 questions) could not be put to the entire population, as scheme of assignments response sheets are not introduced in DEI. However, these findings clearly indicate that there is a need to improve the quality of the assignments in general. As it helps the students in both preparing for the examination as well as in the process of learning, it is for the Distance Education Institute to consider seriously in terms of introducing Response Sheet Assignment without further delay. This requirement is also in line with the philosophy of distance education.

TABLE 4.45
Satisfaction with Quality of Assignments

Are you satisfied with	*OU*				
	Yes		*No*		*Total*
	f	*%*	*f*	*%*	
(a) the quality of questions asked in the assignment?	46	(85.2)	08	(14.8)	54
(b) the quality of work that you are expected to do to respond to the assignment?	46	(82.1)	10	(17.9)	56

4.3.3 Personal Contact Programme (Students' Perception)

The system of distance education in India relies more on face-to-face sessions during personal contact programmers (PCP) than non-contiguous two-way communication through tutor marked assignments for supporting learning of its student. Most of our students on the distance education system have come from the traditional teaching system and have been accustomed to be spoon fed by the teachers teaching in the class room. Similarly, the teachers too are traditional in their approach and feel at ease with lecturing than tutoring through assignment. Thus is the reliance on face-to-face sessions in our distance education system.

In Indian context, distance education students have to complete the given course in a specified period of time and has to take the examination alongwith the regular University

Students, thus, the need for face-to-face contact sessions is justified. Not only this, the UGC guidelines also categorically emphasise that "the provision of Personal Contact Programme should be an essential feature of correspondence education in order that the mind of the student is exposed to the mind of the teachers, tutorials, seminars and other forms of discussion" and recommends that "a contact programme of at least two weeks' duration should be organized in different places, wherever there is a cluster of 200 or more students". The UGC guidelines have not only set the aims of PCPs but have also reflected the *modus operandi* of these programmes.

The term personal contact programme as used in Indian context, denotes the collection of distance students and representative teachers of the supporting institution at a predecided place for a specified period with the intention of supplementing distance learning and teaching. Generally, during this period, there is a face to face encounter between the two which parallels the classroom teaching of the conventional system, only with the difference that in the later the teacher tries to unfold the similar course content in one academic year whereas in the former its unfolding is attempted within a period of two to three weeks.

In this section, the responses of the students regarding suitability of personal contact programme and its academic values are analysed.

Compulsory vs. Voluntary Participation in PCP

The issue whether participation in PCP be compulsory or voluntary is still unresolved in distance education, while some professional bodies like National Council for Teacher Education requires any teacher training programme, B.Ed./M.Ed. offered through distance education mode will have at least 75 percent compulsory attendance in PCP. Distance Education Council, though made it essential for the institutes to organize PCP, encourages students' participation in PCP in large number.

It was therefore thought appropriate to know from the students the present conditions for participation in PCPs and to study their desires if they would like the participation to be made compulsory or voluntary. The results in Table indicate that participation in PCP is compulsory for 30.8 percent students of OU and 16.7 percent students of DEI. Whereas 69.2 percent students of OU feels that participation in PCP is voluntary corresponding to 83.3 percent students of DEI.

Further the students were asked if in their opinion participation in PCPs should be compulsory. It is interesting to note that 49.4 percent students of both the institutes together desires that participation in PCP should be made compulsory. This in itself is an indicator of the fact that PCPs are viewed more positively by a majority of students. Hence the general notion that distance education students, being adults and mostly employed, want independence and autonomy in learning and do not prefer control (say in the form of compulsion to participate in PCP) does not apply to the sample students' population of distance education.

From the Table 4.46 it is seen that 52.5 percent students of DEI as against 42.3 percent students of OU desire that participation in PCPs should be made compulsory. The probable reason for this is that perhaps most of the students of DEI are those school leavers who failed to get admission to conventional colleges because of the problem of limited number of seats available in the colleges. Thus it appears that only 47.5 percent students of DEI and 57.7 percent students of OU who want the participation in PCP to be made voluntary are probably

TABLE 4.46
Participation in PCPs

		Yes		*No*		*Total*
		f	%	*f*	%	
Is the participation in PCPs compulsory in your institute?	DEI	20	(16.7)	100	(83.3)	120
	OU	16	(30.8)	36	(69.2)	52
In your opinion, should the participation in PCPs be compulsory?	DEI	62	(52.5)	56	(47.5)	118
	OU	22	(42.3)	30	(57.7)	52
	Total	84	(49.4)			

employed or adult students including housewives. Whatever may be the facts, but this is an interesting and important area for research, as it has important policy implications as to why participation in PCPs should not be made compulsory when a good majority of students want that.

Suitability of PCPs

The suitability of PCPs implies the suitability of the pace or venue in which it is conducted, the time when they are held and the activities that are organized during the conduct of PCP. Correspondingly three questions were asked to the students. The responses to these questions reveal that the place of PCPs suits 64.0 percent students of OU and 78.0 percent students of DEI and it does not suit to 36.0 percent students of OU and 22 percent students of DEI. The possible reason why the venue of PCP is more suitable to DEI students that OU's is that the PCP centres of IDE are spread throughout the city of Mumbai, providing easy access to almost every students living in the vicinity area. Whereas OU is having a limited number of study centres (only three) and students have to travel from their place of residence to the study centres which could be at a far off place.

Regarding the suitability of time almost equal number of students nearly 60 percent of both OU and DEI indicated that PCPs are organized during the time they really need them and it is not the case of nearly 40 percent students. The data in the Table is self-revealing.

As regards the suitability of activities during the PCP's are concerned, 54.5 percent students of OU and equal percent students of DEI are satisfied with the quality of the activities organized during PCP and 45.5 percent students are not satisfied.

Thus in general it appears that organization of PCPs suits a good majority of students. Nonetheless, it does not suit every third student. Who are these to whom PCPs are not suitable? Do they belong to remote areas? Are they employed? Are they house wives? etc. These are important questions that need further research, as policy implications for organization of PCPs to suit these students can be drawn only when these data are available.

Further, a question was asked as to how many students sit in one class during the conduct of PCP. Varied responses were

TABLE 4.47
Suitability of PCPs

		Yes		No		Total
		f	%	f	%	
Are the PCPs organized at places which suits you?	DEI	92	(78.0)	26	(28.0)	118
	OU	32	(64.0)	18	(36.0)	50
Are the PCPs organized during the time when you really need them?	DEI	66	(56.9)	50	(43.1)	116
	OU	30	(60.0)	20	(40.0)	50
Is the quality of activities during the PCPs satisfactory?	DEI	59	(54.6)	49	(45.4)	108
	OU	24	(54.5)	20	(45.5)	44

received. 85 percent students of OU stated that 25 students sit in one class during the conduct of PCP while 81.7 percent students of DEI stated that on an average 50 students sit in one class during the conduct of PCP and 18.3 percent students stated that more than 100 students sit in one class during PCP.

It is evident from the data that number of students attending PCP classes of IDE are quite large, hence possibly more number of PCP centres are required to be set-up.

Academic Value of PCPs

In order to find out the academic value of PCPs four questions were asked to students which provide ample evidence to judge the academic value of PCPs. The response of the students is given in Table 4.48

From the Table 4.48 it is revealed that more than 80 percent students of OU as well as DEI benefited in their study from the teaching done during the PCP, barely 17.5 percent students reported that they did not benefit in their study from PCPs.

The PCPs are considered worth the time and money spent to attend them by 57.1 percent students, while 42.9 percent students feel that it is not worth spending. Perhaps this is because 67.1 percent students feel that they have not been provided sufficient time for consulting teachers individually to solve their academic problems. Implication of this finding is that students in general do not get much benefit from the PCP lectures rather they need individual counselling. Therefore, a

TABLE 4.48
Academic Value of PCPs

		Yes		No		Total
		f	%	f	%	
Do you benefit in your study from the teaching done during the PCPs?	DEI	87	(80.6)	21	(19.4)	108
	OU	40	(87.0)	06	(13.0)	46
	Total	127	(82.5)	27	(17.5)	154
Is sufficient time provided for consulting individually the teachers of the Institute for academic problems?	DEI	34	(32.1)	72	(67.9)	106
	OU	16	(34.8)	30	(65.2)	46
	Total	50	(32.9)	102	(67.1)	152
Are the PCPs worth the time and money spent to attend them?	DEI	58	(53.7)	50	(46.3)	108
	OU	30	(65.2)	16	(34.8)	46
	Total	88	(57.1)	66	(42.9)	154
Do the PCPs serve the purpose of removing your academic problems?	DEI	74	(67.3)	36	(32.7)	110
	OU	34	(73.9)	12	(26.1)	46
	Total	108	(69.2)	48	(30.8)	156

very clear cut implication is that during the PCPs around 50 percent time should be given to face-to-face teaching and 50 percent to individual consultation by students to get their personal and academic problems solved.

However, if we go further in analysing the question whether PCPs serve the purpose of removing your academic problems, it is interesting to note that 69.2 percent students reported that PCPs help them in removing their academic problems while 30.8 percent students have their reservations. This finding suggests that on the whole PCPs are benefiting the student, they can still be more beneficial if individual interaction with the teachers is arranged and more individualized tutoring is introduced in addition to face-to-face teaching. This is an important implication from the point of view of managing the PCPs.

The students were further asked if audio-video cassettes were shown to them during PCP. It is observed from Table 4.49 that only 16.7 percent students have stated that they have been shown audio-video cassettes during PCP while a majority of 83.3 percent students stated that they have not been shown audio and video cassettes. It is therefore suggested that a fair amount of audio and video programmes be screened during the conduct of PCP which will benefit the students. The findings of this study is in line with earlier studies conducted which stated that facilities at study centres especially audio-video programmes are underutilised to the extent than even many students are not aware of such facilities at the study centres (Harichandan, 1993)

TABLE 4.49
Audio and Video Shows during PCP

		Yes		*No*		*Total*
		f	%	*f*	%	
Are you shown Audio/Video Cassettes during PCP?	DEI	13	(12.5)	91	(87.5)	104
	OU	12	(26.1)	34	(73.9)	46
	Total	25	(16.7)	125	(83.3)	150

Seeing the overall results in this section it is the firm conviction of the investigator that if PCPs are organized in a way as discussed, then it will prove to be of optimum value of supplementing distance study.

The students gave the following suggestions in response to an open ended question to improve the PCPs:

Suggestions of the Students

(i) Most of the students wanted that number of days for organising PCPs should be increased from 6 to 7 PCPs to atleast 10 PCPs in each session be organised.

(ii) Students of DEI felt that PCPs should start early. To organise PCPs in the month of January for the examination to be held in March/April does not serve any purpose as is being done currently in DEI.

(iii) Students of DEI expressed that PCPs should be organised in every subject rather than in a selected number of subjects.

(iv) Subject specialists (experts be deputed to conduct PCPs) and they should give more time for discussion than teaching alone.

(v) More number of teachers should be involved and students should be divided into small groups according to their needs and assigned to teachers separately, so that individualized tutoring is possible.

(vi) All PCPs should be completed at least two months before the examinations and students should not be disturbed by asking them to participate in the PCPs just before the examination.

(vii) Most of the students of DEI as well as OU felt that PCPs should be made compulsory.

Although students gave a number of other suggestions, the above noted suggestions are selected, because they reflect important management implications, pertaining to the time, duration of PCPs and experts to be involved in organising PCP.

4.3.4 Study Centre (Students' Perception)

Being separated from the institutions , the distance learner fails to get immediate feedback from the teachers, lacks access to good library to supplement his studies and suffers the feelings of learning in isolation, i.e. he does not get opportunity to interact with his fellow students and the staff of his supporting institution.

As we have already seen earlier, the disadvantages of immediate feedback is attempted to be compensated to some extent by (a) providing delayed feedback through non-contiguous two-way communication in the form of written assignments as well as study materials prepared in self-instructional format ; and (b) face to face teaching, counselling, tutoring, etc. during personal contact programmes, but these helps alone are not adequate to put the distance learner in the same parlour as the one enjoyed by the regular students. Further, the lack of library facilities and felling of isolation remains. Thus, the distance education institutes have to constantly strive to minimize these disadvantages still they are completely eliminated. In this effort the system of the study centres and providing in them certain support services like library and other media facilities, tutoring, counselling, etc. has come to be widely recognised as a major input in supporting distance education.

Study Centre in a miniature extension of the supporting distance education institutes into a locality where there is a good concentration of its students. Normally a study centre should be equipped with :

(a) a small library having relevant books, reference materials and study materials, journals, etc.;
(b) audio-video cassettes, film slides, film strips along with electronic gadget to play them;
(c) a computer terminal;
(d) adequate facilities for sitting, reading and writing work; and
(e) staffed by a team of part time or full time subject tutors/counsellors.

The Study Centres act both as a resource centre and support centre in the vicinity of the distance learners.

Since there is always a possibility of finding other fellow students in the Study Centres, the isolated learner gets an opportunity to interact with them. Often the supporting distance education institutes keep Study Centres as venues for PCP, examinations and other get together programmes, thus providing excellent opportunities for removing learners' isolation. With this picture and functions of Study Centres in mind, an attempt has been made in this section to find out the facilities provided and the extent of their utility by the students.

Reporting Study Centre Facility

It was found that 96.4 percent students of OU indicated that the institute provided Study Centre facilities where as only 3.6 percent students replied in negative. In case of DEI 84.8 percent students indicated that the institute provided Study Centre facilities to them in the form of PCP centres. However, 15.2 percent students indicated that the institute does not provided study centre facilities. This could be due to the fact that although DEI does not have the concept of study centre, they do have PCP centres. Probably these students have confused PCP centres as study centres.

Distance and Timing of Study Centre

The distance and the opening timing of the Study Centre are particularly important, as they determine the convenience

TABLE 4.50

Number of Students Reporting Study Centre Facility

		Yes		No		Total
		f	%	f	%	
Does your institute provide Study Centre facility to you?	DEI	89	(84.8)	16	(15.2)	105
	OU	56	(96.4)	02	(3.6)	56
	Total	143	(88.8)	18	(11.2)	161

with which the students can come to make use of the facilities in the Study Centres. An enquiry about the distance of the Study Centres from the residence of the students was made. The data presented in Table 4.51 reveals that 38.7 percent students had their Study Centres within the radius of 10 kilometres. Whereas for 31.7 percent students the Study Centre was within a distance of 10 to 30 kilometres, and for 18.3 percent students the Study Centre was within a distance of 30-50 kilometres. This means that almost 88.7 percent (38.7 + 31.7 + 18.3 Percent) students could travel daily, if so desired, from their residence to the study centre to make use of the facilities there. In a metropolitan city like Mumbai a distance of 50 kilometres can be covered through the use of suburban train services within one and half an hour. For the remaining 11.3 percent students, the distance was 50 to 100 kilometres for 9.9 percent students and more than 100 kilometres for 1.4 percent students.

This implies that for students beyond 50 kiliometres away

TABLE 4.51

Distance of Study Centre

How far is the Study Centre from your residence?	*DEL*		*OU*		*Total*	
(i) Upto 10 kms.	35	(39.8)	20	(37.0)	55	(38.7)
(ii) 11 to 30 kms.	27	(30.7)	18	(33.3)	45	(31.7)
(iii) 31 to 50 kms.	14	(15.9)	12	(22.2)	26	(18.3)
(iv) 51 to 100 kms.	10	(15.9)	04	(7.4)	14	(9.9)
(v) 101 kms. and above	02	(2.3)		—	02	(1.4)
Total	88		54		142	

from the study centres, it would be possible only on weekends to come to study centres and that too not very often.

As regends the opening timings of the study centres are concerned the students reported of timing which ranges from 4 p.m. to 8 p.m. Regarding suitability of the opening timing of the study centre, it was revealed that the opening timings of the study centres, suits 68.5 percent students and it does not suit 31.5 percent students.

TABLE 4.52
Suitability of Opening Time of Study Centres

		Yes		*No*		*Total*
		f	*%*	*f*	*%*	
Does the opening time of study centres suit you ?	DEI	64	(71.9)	25	(28.1)	89
	OU	34	(63.0)	20	(37.0)	54
	Total	98	(68.5)	45	(31.5)	143

As regends the frequency of opening of study centres are concerned, it was indicated by 80.0 percent students that the student centre remains open everyday, 16.7 percent students reported that the study centres remain open twice in a week and only 3.3 percent students reported that it remain open once in a week.

TABLE 4.53
Frequency of Opening of Study Centres

The study centre remains open	*DEL*		*OU*		*Total*	
(i) Every day	64	(84.2)	32	(72.7)	96	(80.0%)
(ii) Twice in a week	10	(13.2)	10	(22.7)	20	(16.7%)
(iii) Once in a week	02	(2.6)	02	(4.5)	04	(3.3%)
Total					120	

Frequency of Visits to Study Centres

It was considered important to study the frequency with

which the students visit study centres for supplementing their studies, as it would indicate the frequency of utilisations of facilities at the study centres. The data in Table 4.54 reveals that 55.4 percent students of DEI visited study centres to use the services provided there once in a week, while none of the OU students visited study centres on every day basis, 22.9 percent students visited study centres once in a week, 36.5 percent students visited study centres once in a month and 6.3 percent students rarely visited study centres. Who are these students who rarely visits study centre? Are they those for whom the study centres are more than 100 kms away from their residence? If it is so, then the implication is to provide study centres in their neighbourhood. For financial reasons, this may not be possible, thus it is suggested that some residential facility at the study centre may be provided for students coming from distance places.

TABLE 4.54
Frequency of Visits to Study Centres

How often do you visit the study centres to use the services provided there ?	*DEL*		*OU*		*Total*	
(i) Every day	31	(55.4)	—		31	(32.3)
(ii) Once in a week	12	(21.4)	10	(25.0)	22	(22.9)
(iii) Once in 15 days	—		02	(5.0)	02	(2.1)
(iv) Once in a month	09	(7.1)	26	(65.0)	35	(36.5)
(v) Rarely	04	(7.1)	02	(5.0)	06	(6.3)
Total	56		40		96	

Services Utilised

In this section the utilisation of services as reported by students have been examined. Students were asked what type of services provided in the study centre were utilised by you without giving any clue of the services provided at the study centres. The responses of the students are analysed in Table 4.55.

TABLE 4.55
Services Utilised at Study Centres

Services Utilised	*DEI*		*OU*		*Total*	
Teaching	12	(46.2)	04	(25.0)	16	(38.0)
Library	11	(42.3)	08	(50.0)	19	(45.2)
Consultation	03	(11.5)	02	(12.5)	05	(11.9)
Information		—	02	(12.5)	02	(4.8)
Total	26		16		42	

It is observed that 45.2 percent students use the services of library followed by teaching (38.0 percent). Though consultation with the tutor is the third most frequently used services at the study centres by about 12 percent students, it is interesting to note that the study centres are equally used for discussions and meeting with fellow students. Thus, it can be safely concluded that study centres do play an important role in removing the learner isolation besides other academic role. It is also pertinent to note that students of DEI do not ask for any information at the study centres since dissemination of information is centralised at the headquarters only. However, 12.5 percent students of OU use the services of information from the study centre.

Now the students were presented a list of eight possible services offered at the study centres and were asked to tick mark the one's that were used by them and give a rank 1, 2, 3 . . . . 8, etc., according to the extent of frequency used. Rank one indicated most frequently used and rank 8 indicated least frequently used. By using SPSS package in the computer through cross-tabulation, it was observed that face to face teaching continues to get first priority by about 65.9 percent students. The use of library facilities comes at the second place. Though counselling with tutor for personal/administrative problem is the third most frequently used services followed by discussion and meeting with fellow students with fourth rank. Other services utilised by the students in the study centres are given in that order of priority as fifth rank-counselling with the tutor for academic problem, sixth rank—use of computer, seventh rank—audio tape and eighth rank—video/films.

TABLE 4.56
Ranking of the Facilities at Study Centres

Which of the following services provided at the study centre do you frequently make use of it ?	*Rank*	*Score*
(i) Counselling with tutor for personal/ administrative problem	3	54.1
(ii) Counselling with tutor for academic problems	5	37.3
(iii) Library facility	2	61.3
(iv) Audio tapes	7	26.1
(v) Video/Films	8	20.8
(vi) Computer	6	36.2
(vii) Discussion and meeting with fellow students	4	52.8
(viii) Face to face teaching (P.C.P.)	1	65.9

Students' Satisfaction

Seven measures of students' satisfaction were taken as criteria for evaluating the effectiveness of the services provided at the study centres. The students' responses to the seven corresponding questions presented in Table 4.57 revealed that 58.5 percent students are satisfied with their tutor and the tutorial help received by them, whereas 41.5 percent students are not satisfied. While 85.4 percent students agreed about the library facilities at the study centre, only 14.6 percent replied in negative. In the opinion of the 56.8 percent students, the library facilities are not adequate for meeting the learning needs. Only in the case of 43.2 percent students the library of the study centre is having adequate facilities. While 51 percent students reported that the study centre library does not have the facility of borrowing of books, 49 percent students reported the facility of borrowing of books.

60.7 percent students reported that they have free access to the books and journals in the library at study centre, whereas 39.3 percent did not have free access to them. As far as audio/ video tapes and other electronic media at the study centers are concerned, only 17.7 percent students reported that they can use these facilities at the study centers. In the case of 82.3 percent students, it may be possible that their study centers do not have such facilities or they do not have free access to them. Both the situations are undesirable and should receive adequate attention of the planners' administrators, as distance education without the support of electronic media these days is almost like external/private study.

On the whole 60 percent students are satisfied with the overall facilities provided at the study centers and 40.0 percent are on the whole not satisfied with the facilities provided in their study centers. This finding implies that there is still a lot of scope for providing facilities and improving the functioning of the study centers.

TABLE 4.57
Some Measures of Students' Satisfaction

Measures of Satisfaction		*Yes*		*No*		*Total*
		f	%	*f*	%	
Are you satisfied with	DEI	46	(56.1)	36	(43.9)	82
your tutor and the	OU	30	(62.5)	18	(37.5)	48
tutorial services?	Total	76	(58.5)	54	(41.5)	130
Do you have library facilities	DEI	77	(81.1)	18	(18.9)	95
at your study centre?	OU	52	(92.9)	04	(7.1)	56
	Total	129	(85.4)	22	(14.6)	151
Are the library facilities	DEI	53	(51.5)	50	(48.5)	103
adequate for meeting your	OU	14	(26.9)	38	(73.1)	52
learning needs?	Total	67	(43.2)	88	(56.8)	155
Do you have the facility of	DEI	61	(64.2)	34	(35.8)	95
borrowing books?	OU	12	(22.2)	42	(77.8)	54
	Total	73	(49.0)	76	(51.0)	149
Do you have free access to	DEI	58	(63.7)	33	(36.3)	91
the books and journals in the	OU	30	(55.6)	24	(44.4)	54
library at the study centre?	Total	88	(60.7)	57	(39.3)	145
Do you freely use the audio/	DEI	15	(17.2)	72	(82.8)	87
video tape at the study centre?	OU	10	(18.5)	44	(81.5)	54
	Total	25	(17.7)	116	(82.3)	141
On the whole are you satisfied	DEI	49	(53.8)	42	(46.2)	54
with the overall facilities	OU	38	(70.4)	16	(29.6)	91
provided at the study centre?	Total	87	(60.0)	58	(40.0)	145

Finally, in the light of the above findings, the students were assumed to give source open suggestions for the improvement of study centre facilities.

Although a various of suggestions were put forth by the students, however, only those considered important from the point of view of their practicability and those pointed out by a majority of students are listed above.

SUGGESTIONS FOR IMPROVEMENT

The last question in the students' questionnaire pertains to some open suggestions for the improvement of study centre facilities. Although a variety of suggestions were put forth by the students, only those considered important from the point of view of their practicability and those pointed out by a majority of students are listed below :

(i) Most students suggested that the opening time of study centres should suit the working people and its timing should be increased.
(ii) In the study centre library more number of reference books and books of latest edition should be available alongwith some journals.
(iii) The facility of borrowing books from the library of study centres should be introduced and provision of issuing at least 2 to 3 books, which the students can retain.
(iv) Audio and video centre should be improved.
(v) One very interesting suggestion was that fees and forms be submitted at the study centre and study centres should act as a single window system for every thing.

PART 3

4.4 PRACTICES OF STUDENT SUPPORT SERVICES ABROAD

This part deals with the latest practices, innovations and world trends adopted in distance teaching systems elsewhere particularly in European context where the first Open University in the world was established. The two institutions identified are the United Kingdom Open University and the European Association of Distance Teaching Universities. This part deals with the third objective of the study and the corresponding research question which are stated below.

Objective 3

"To find out the provision of Student Support Services with the latest practices, innovations and world trends adopted in distance teaching systems elsewhere and suggest improvement".

Research Question 3

What are the latest practices and trends adopted in distance education systems elsewhere with respect to Student Support Services and their possible adaptation?

4.4.1 Support Services in EADTU

The European Association of Distance Teaching Universities (EADTU) consisting of 17 member organisations from 15 European countries was established in January 1987 with a mission to promote and support the creation of European Network of higher level distance education. The European Open University Network (EOUN) has been established in 1992 as the executive arm of the EADTU which supports member institutions in relation to projects contributing toward the creation of European Open University Network. The major instrument of EOUN is the establishment of an Europe wide network of Euro Study Centres (ESC) to give access to open learning courses from institutions in all European countries and provide for the student support services.

Functions of EOUN Service Centres

The main functions of the EOUN service centres are :

- It is a documentation centre in which all relevant material and documentation on distance teaching are stored and made available to the various Euro Study Centres. This documentation centre serves both as a central database and as an assembly point of all relevant information. The documentation centre is accessible through telematic networks or by visiting the centre.

- It works as an experimental laboratory where new ideas are set-up and facilitates relevant for the Euro Study Centres are tested, converted for specific use and/or adapted to the specific environments of the Euro Study Centres.
- It facilitates and supports implementation of the appropriate quality assurance criteria to be represented by the Euro Study Centre logo. An important role of the Euro Study Centres is to define and meet the quality approaches necessary for the delivery of high quality distance mode education programmes. The existing EADTU member already have such nationally based systems. The evolution of European standards will underpin future co-operation and activities within the EOUN. Such procedures will be based on self-evaluation approaches, supplemented by peer group visits and other contacts.
- It is a training centre for Euro Study Centre managers and teachers.
- It facilitates the management of networking and co-operation among the Euro Study Centres. This Network function may vary from organising mutual events and exchanges of information and experiences between existing Euro Study Centres, to activities related to the extension of the network to other areas of interest, organisations and markets.
- It provides consultancy services for new or existing centres through the various instruments like co-operation between an existing Euro Study Centre and a newly established Euro Study Centre, the provision of start-up management either provided by the service centres or by one of the study centres, project planning and fund raising for new Euro Study Centres.

Euro Study Centres

The major instrument of the EOUN is the establishment of a Europe-wide network of Euro Study Centres. This local or regional provision aims to demonstrate the potential of open distance learning, give access to these courses from institutions in all European countries and provide for the indispensable Student Support Services. Euro Study centres are established in existing facilities like the local study centres of the open universities or open and flexible learning centres of traditional universities. It can also be established as new facilities, in joint ventures with open and distance learning organisations, local authorities and industry. Euro Study Centres are selected through a process of self-assessment and peer group review, based on agreed quality criteria for self-staff profile, learning facilities, telematic network access and European awareness. Forty-three Euro Study Centres have been established during 1995, the first year of operation of the network. These locally based Euro Study Centres are linked to the providers of open distance learning by telematic networks which facilitates the European transfer of distance course information, course materials and provides for trans European student support services.

Functions of Euro Study Centres

The Major functions of Euro Study Centres are to:

- Provide information and documentation service;
- Facilitate foreign course enrolment and international credit transfer point;
- Provide support services for delivery of European course programmes;
- Provide information and counselling about joint EADTU courses; and
- Organise specialised tutoring services, etc.

4.4.2 Support Services in UKOU

The support services of UKOU are provided through the 13 Regional Centres and 293 Study Centres spread throughout the UK. There are about 7,300 part-time tutorial and counselling staff. Although students learn at home, there is plenty of support and human contact available to them. Every new undergraduate student is assigned to a local tutor-counsellor for their first year's study. The combined role of tutor-counsellor at this stage is based on the belief that many inexperienced adult students need a high level of support early on their Open University Studies. After the foundation year, students are assigned to specialist tutor appropriate to their courses. Their tutor-counsellor, however, remains with them as their counsellor and primary contact with the university, to advise on study problems and on longer-term educational plans.

Study centres are located in other educational establishments. They are used for students and their tutors to meet for a variety of face-to-face evening tutorials and day schools usually held on Saturdays. Short residential schools are also organised for many kinds of Open University study. They are arranged in other universities during their vacation periods, conference centres and hotels.

The regional services are a vital link in the university's line of communication with students and tutorial and counselling staff. Each region has a committee which brings together students, tutorial and counselling staff and full-time staff.

The university also has a central consultative committee which includes one student and one part-time staff member from each region. These original committees give student tutors and counselling staff the opportunity to comment on university activities and initiative and to feed ideas into the open university decision-making process. They provide a direct channel of communication from every study centre to the university headquarters.

Each region operates an enquiry and admission service which is the first link between new or potential students and the university. They give advice about the open university's courses, facilities available and information on other study opportunities available locally. Most open university courses are now available in other European countries. For them, local support is provided under the direction of selected Regional Centres. There are currently about 8,000 students studying with the U.K. Open University in Europe.

One of the glaring fact of UKOU is the extension of specialised support services to the disabled students. It is a policy of UKOU to encourage disabled people to study with the Open University and to provide them with the necessary support and facilities to do so on equal terms with open students wherever possible. The university has developed a wide range of services to meet the special educational needs of disabled students. The office coordinates these for students with disabilities. These services include: identification of special needs, counselling, tuition, study centre allocation, preparatory courses, special learning materials, equipments, summer school support, specialised information, etc.

The support system, providing linking between materials and learning included atleast nine interlocking components, many of which were optional to the students. These structures came under the control of the UKOU's Regional Tutorial Services department and were described by Sewart (1978) as a continuity of concern for the student studying at a distance :

- The tutor-counsellor who follows the student throughout his university career.
- The tutor available for consultation on an individual score.
- 13 regional offices providing a decentralised focus for the administration of tuition, counselling and student support systems.
- A study centre within easy travelling distance where the student can meet other students and use facilities.
- Tutorials at regular intervals.
- Computerised student records that can pick up problems in students progress and anticipate dropout.
- Kosmat analysis a computerised weighting of the grades given by tutors on all assignments against the national average.
- Residential summer schools.
- A student association with regional branches.

4.4.3 Quality Assurance System and Support Services in EADTU and UKOU

Quality assurance is a crucial aspect of distance education

system. Each component of distance education demands stringent adherence of standardised procedure to provide error-free products or services. Guri (1993), has expressed the same view that Distance Teaching Universities have had to prove that the education they offer is valuable and on a high level and even more qualitative in some respects, as compared to some conventional universities. Support services are the fore-front of the system; hence, a well knitted mechanism is inevitable to ensure qualitative support services to the distant learners. Undoubtedly, it depends on the quality of other components of distance education system. Broadly the components of distance education may be divided into two major areas. First, the planning, development and production of multimedia package, and second, the delivery of the distance education. Hence, the quality needs to be continuously maintained at each stage of planning, production, delivery and support services of the distant teaching materials. Deshpande (1994), has focussed that the quality assurance trends in higher education seem to be universally consistent in respect of the purpose and approach in most of the Commonwealth and European Countries.

Euro study centres, the sub-system of EOUN, is an upto date delivery system for distance education and training across the European countries. ESC can be described in terms of its educational and training facilities; the telecommunication and data processing facilities; its European dimension, a tool for fostering virtual mobility as well as its impact on human resources development in the Regions. Specifically in the area of quality assurance, EADTU members have chosen an approach of self-assessent and peer review by ESCs. A format/manual has been developed to produce self-study reports which is integrated in the process of internal evaluation. The main purpose is to contribute to local quality improvement and to create an effective process of self-improvement.

Euro study centre staff development is another landmark of EADTU. This is one of the important services offered to ESC network members by the EOUN service centre. The overall aim of staff development is to support the realisation of ESC network and the aims set for the network of transnational study centres. ESC staff development is a dynamic process which takes into account existing knowledge and skills of study centre

Staff. On the other hand, it also tries to anticipate new skills and knowledge requirements needed in study centres which are operating on the European level. In fact, in this process trainees are constantly evaluating and defining new needs for their training. Staff development is seen as a key element of creating operational network of Euro study centres. This is done by offering continuous staff development activities after the Study centre has joined the ESC network. The programmes of staff development are carried out by : self-study, seminars, workshops, electronic conferences, visits, staff exchange, etc. UK has developed a strong mechanism of quality assurance. In UKOU the quality is maintained through training of writers, agreeing specification for a material with all intrested parties including profesional bodies, use of external reviewers, field testing with staff and students, staff development and support in the use of materials and the implementation of open learning by members. At the delivery point responsibility for quality rests with the member institutions.

UKOU has established a Quality Support Centre (QSC) for the maintenance and enhancement of quality in higher education. It provides services to higher education institutions and to quality assurance and assessment agencies in the UK and internationally. The work of QSC falls into two main areas, i.e. systems and methods of quality assurance, assessment and management and relationship between higher education and the world of work. Within each area QSC continues to undertake research/development projects, provide consultancy, produce publications and run workshops and conferences.

The regional staff of UKOU constitute front line troops for improving the retention of students through a commitment to deliver quality support. The university is continuously involved in raising quality standards and refining the ways in which support is delivered. The planning for change goes hand in hand with the maintenance of the day-to-day operations of that region. The university invests significant amount in the training and development of Regional Directors, their Deputies and Regional Secretaries in aspects of change management such as communication and human resource development as they have to lead their staff in providing effective services in the changing scenario. A residential conference of senior counsellors held at

Asfon University was a significant step in refocussing this valued staff category on the integrated student support service which is to be introduced from 1996 onwards.

4.4.4 Salient Features of European Support Services

On the basis of the above discussion the major features of European Support Services are:

- Efficient documentation centre.
- Wide role of various units involved in support services.
- Active involvement in research and development activities by Regional and Study Centres.
- Easy accessibility to these units of support services by students.
- Efficient procedures of international credit transfer.
- Active involvement of these centres in the promotional activities.
- Strong co-ordination among Headquarters, Regional Centres and Study Centres.

4.4.5 Implications of European Support Services for OU and DEI in India

Strong and effective support services are the backbone of the distance education system. Hence, continuous and intense efforts are needed to provide quality support services to the distance learners. Indian distance education system has also followed the system of Regional and Study Centres. Based on European model of distance support system, there is a dire need of strengthening Regional and Study Centres. The activities need to be decentralized upto the Study Centres.

The efficient delivery mechanism demands the gap of production of services and the use of services to be bridged. This requires an efficient mechanism of unfettered flow of information to the distance learners. Study centres may work as a documentation centre where all informations are to be made readily available. Strong coordination among Headquarter, Electronic Media Production Centre, Regional Centres, Study Centres facilitate the process of smooth discharge of services upto the end users.

Intense Marketing and promotional measures are to be carried out by these centres. Being in direct contact with the clients, they should be actively involved in the feedback process and research and development of distance mode of education. This is the ripe time for the Indian distance education system to follow a continuous feedback mechanism for further improvement of the system. The system of quality assurance ensures standard learning materials and reliable delivery services. The University immediately requires to incorporate the quality assurance mechanism in each component of distance education system. A Quality Support Centre may be established to ensure qualitative product and efficient delivery system. The quality assurance mechanism any be embedded in each stage of the distance education system. Peer Group evaluation strategy may be adopted for the continuous improvement of the learning materials.

The distance education system needs to evolve an effective mechanism of movement of students from conventional system to distance system and *vice-versa*. This requires efficient mechanism of transfer of credit so that students may be easily accommodated from one system to another one.

OU and DEI may establish study centres beyond the country based on the global operations of European study centres. In fact, the University has already initiated the process of establishing study centres in Dubai and Abudhabi. The rapid use of Teleconferencing and other electronic media may immensely facilitate imparting distance education beyond the country.

Another important area is the development of persons involved in the preparation and delivery of the distance education system. Koul (1992) has highlighted that proper and adequate staff development scheme in distance education techniques and in the methods of open learning for all staff are essential to maximize the efficiency, effectiveness and quality of its teaching/learning. A wide range of developmental programmes are required for the improvement of persons involved in the production and delivery of learning materials. Trained manpower provides efficient delivery services to large number of distant learners. Hence, immediate attention is needed for the adequate development of all kinds of staff engaged in this process.

Support Services play a pivotal role in the distance education system. Effective delivery mechanism requires strong coordination among all components of delivery system. Continuous research and feedback mechanism are needed for the further improvement of the system. This has become more pertinent because globalization has also entered into the academic arena. As a result, several foreign academic institutions have already started imparting education through distance mode in India. Certainly, Distance institutions will face severe competition with these well satisfying the large number of distant learners and competing with these mushrooming world level distance teaching institutions.

PART 4

4.5 COMPARISON OF STUDENT SUPPORT SERVICES: CONVENTIONAL AND OPEN UNIVERSITY

This part is an attempt to compare the provision of Student Support Services of Conventional University with that of Open University with an intention to improve upon the facilities provided by the dual mode conventional education system and to develop some kind of framework/model for Student Support Services in a conventional set-up. This part deals with the fourth and last objective of the study and the corresponding research question. The same is stated below.

Objective 4

"To compare the existing Student Support Services with the Conventional and Open University and suggest improvement".

Research Question 4

Why is there a perceived thinking of better provision of Student Support Services in Open University than Conventional System?

It has been observed that of the four essential components

of Students Support Services identified, only two are available in the Distance Education Institute, i.e. Study Material and Personal Contact Programme. Even Study Materials are neither in self instructional format nor upto the standard as revealed by the students. Most importantly the two major components of Student Support Services which every Distance Education Institute must provide, i.e. system of Assignment Response Sheet and Study Centres are conspicuously absent in the Distance Education Institute.

It is therefore, very strongly felt that the Distance Education Institute must introduce the concept of continuous assessment by introducing assignment.

5

Summary and Conclusions

5.1 INTRODUCTION

Student Support Services have now become an integral part of most of the good Distance Education Institutes, particularly in the Open Universities but Distance Education Institutes are yet to catch up with the trend. Today, it is a recognized and accepted fact/norm that adequate Student Support Services are provided to the distance learners who are most of the time, studying in isolation, away from the institution, teachers and fellow students. The purpose is to help the students overcome the feeling of isolation and to facilitate learning through.

- Carefully prepared Study Materials in the self-instructional format in simple language, with clear cut objectives, good content coverage with illustrations, self-check exercises, a summary at the end, a glossary of difficult and technical words and a list of suggested readings.
- Appropriate constructive comments on the

performance of students so as to encourage and help them on developing two way didactic communication through comments on assignments.

- Organising Personal Contact Programme lectures by intensive face to face classroom teaching, individual guidance and counselling, encouraging regular study habits and instill confidence in students.
- The system of Study Centres and providing in them support services, like library and audio-video facilities, tutoring, counselling, etc.

Friedman commented at an early stage of modern distance education that the emphasis within the field as service to students was unusual for an academic institution (Friedman, 1981). However, while there has subsequently appeared a substantial literature as methodologies relating to the production of learning materials and resources for open and distance learning relatively little has been written about the planning and management of Student Support Services.

5.2 SUMMARY

With this background in view, the present study is aimed at studying the present practices of Student Support Services as is available in the Distance Education Institute and Open University in India and the perception of the students about the Student Support Services. It also aims at studying the trends available in some of the leading Open Universities of the world for possible adaptation of their practices in Indian context and drawing conclusions for improving the existing scenario. A study of the Student Support Services of Distance Education Institute and Open University is also attempted in the present study.

Statement of the Problem

The problem under investigation in the present study is entitled as :

> "A Study of Student Support Services in Distance Education Institute of Conventional University and Open University".

Objectives of the Study

The specific objectives of the study are as follows :

- To study the present practices adopted for Student Support Services in Distance Education Institute and Open University with respect to: (a) study material, (b) assignment, (c) personal contact programme, and (d) study centre.
- To critically study the provision of Student Support Services from learner's point of view and the perception of the students.
- To find out the provision of Student Support Services with the latest practices, innovations and world trends adopted in distance teaching systems elsewhere.
- To compare the existing support services with the conventional and Open University and suggest improvement.

Methodology of the Study

Survey method was used for investigation, as this was found to be the most appropriate method to survey the present practices of Student Support Services prevailing in the Conventional University as well as Open University. Qualitative research was also used as the basis for generating models and frameworks based upon the practices of Student Support Services.

The two institutions selected for the study are the Institute of Distance Education, University of Mumbai (one of the oldest Universities in the country) and Indira Gandhi National Open University (the first National Open University) besides the association of the researcher with these institutions were the other factors of selection of these two institutes.

A total number of 176 students constitute the sample for the present study which were drawn by systematic sampling procedure from a population of 2700 students through postal questionnaire.

The tools used for the present study include two sets of questionnaires: one for the Director and Coordinator and the other for the students. Besides, observation schedule was developed and used while visiting the institutions for the purpose of this study. These questionnaires were personally administered by the researcher to the Director and Coordinator of the institute.

The present study used simple statistical techniques such as frequency and percentage. In addition, most of the data were interpreted through the method of descriptive analysis and wherever necessary cross-tabulations have been generated.

5.3 MAJOR FINDINGS OF THE STUDY

5.3.1 Study Materials : DEI

In the Distance Education Institute the study materials are written by individual teachers from the constituent colleges. In the DEI, a panel of course writers is prepared. Expertise and specialization are the main criteria for the selection of course writers. Although guidelines are sent to the lesson writers, hardly any orientation programmes are organised to train them for writing lessons in the distance education format and more particularly in self-instructional style. Course writers have no training in self-instructional materials.

- Proof reading of the lessons is done by subject experts. There is no involvement of language editor, media expert, and educational technologist in the preparation of study materials.
- Figures, diagrams, charts, tables, illustrations and examples are conspicuously absent in the study materials of DEI.
- There is complete absence of intext questions (self-check exercises, or check your progress) and the lessons are not written according to the principles of self-learning materials.
- Even the typography has not been appropriately set and there are many spelling mistakes in the study materials.
- In the DEI, the study materials are mostly hand delivered in one lot to the students at the time of admissions and sometimes the study materials are not available as per the requirements of the students.

- The study materials once developed are not subject to any kind of evaluation in DEI for judging its didactic suitability for distance education students.
- Study material is not prepared in all the subjects that the DEI offers to its students.
- The content is not presented in an intimate personal style, most of the presentation being in the usual textbook style.

5.3.2 Study Material : OU

- In Open University the Study materials are written by the faculty of the university, teachers from other Universities and also by course teams. The faculty of the University and outside experts constitute the course team.
- In the OU content editing is done by course editors, language editing is done by the faculty and language editors and format editing is done by the Distance Education Specialists. Proof reading of the course units is done by the academic staff and the University proof readers.
- The study materials are in self-instructional format with adequate figures and diagrams, intext questions and suggested further readings.
- In OU study materials are sent by Registered post in instalments. A schedule for the dispatch of the study materials is also sent to the students and they have been able to stick to the schedule.
- The study materials are prepared in all the subjects that OU offers to its students.
- The study materials of OU are evaluated by inviting criticism of subject experts in the field and by following some standard guidelines.
- The content structure, aims and objectives and introduction, all these access devices in the beginning of the unit are immensely helpful to the students.
- Study materials should be prepared in other languages and latest developments be included instead of reprint the old version.

- On the whole the students found the course materials of OU not only self-instructional but also helpful in understanding the topics.
- Study materials should have colour diagrams, charts, and contemporary examples and list of reference books.

5.3.3 Assignments

- The system of submission of Assignments have not yet been introduced in DEI.
- In Open University, submission of Assignment Response sheets is compulsory and they count towards internal assessment. It is a requirement for writing the term end examination.
- In OU students are required to submit 3 assignments per course and 3 months time is given for submission of assignments.
- The purpose of assignment is continuous assessment of students' performance and giving feedback to the students for improvement.
- Tutor comments on the assignments are written personally pointing out the individual mistakes.
- On the whole students are satisfied with the comments written on their assignments.
- Submission of assignments help in the process of learning as well as preparing for the examination.
- Students are satisfied with the quality of questions asked in the assignment.
- Students have reported that if model answers are sent alongwith the assessed assignment, then it helps in the process of learning and also in preparing for the examination.
- Assignments are assessed by the part time counsellors in the study centres.
- There are Tutor Marked Assignments (TMA) as well as Computer Marked Assignments (CMA).
- Both the grading and marking systems have been introduced in OU.
- Most of the students of OU found the submission of assignments helpful in clarifying concepts, etc., and in improving their performance in the final examination.

5.3.4 Personal Contact Programme in DEI

- In Distance Education Intitute, PCPs are organised for a period of 3 months in a year towards the end of the course and just before the commencement of the examinations. It is held on everyday except Sunday between 6.00 p.m. to 8.00 p.m.
- PCPs are organised in the constituent colleges and the faculty of the colleges are the resource persons.
- The main aim of PCPs is to formally teach the content to the students through face to face classroom teaching.
- PCPs help in supplementing the study materials and preparing for the examination.
- Students are not shown audio video cassettes during PCP
- Though participation in PCP is voluntary, still large number of students turn up for attending the PCP Classes.
- PCP classes of DEI are over crowded.
- More number of teachers should be invited for PCP and the students should be divided into small groups.
- Normally six to seven lectures are arranged in each course.
- Students of Distance Education Institute feel that PCPs should start early and the number of PCPs should be increased to at least 10 in each course.
- Sufficient time is not provided for consulting individual teachers of the institute.
- PCPs should be organised in all the subjects rather than in selected subjects as is being practised currently.
- All PCPs should be completed at least two months prior to the commencement of examination.
- Most of the students of Distance Education Institute as well as Open University feel that PCPs should be made compulsory.

5.3.5 Personal Contact Programme in OU

- Duration of PCPs in Open University is 6 months in a year during March to May and September to November (i.e. beginning and towards end of the year). It is held only on Sundays.

- PCPs are organised in the study centres and six lectures are arranged in each course.
- Nature of participation in PCP is voluntary, though on an average 15 to 20 students attend PCP classes.
- The main objective behind organising PCP in the OU is to remove the learning difficulties and to provide individual tutoring and counselling to the students.
- PCPs help in removing the academic problems and encourages the students to put forward their academic and personal problems.
- Timing, place and activities organised under PCP are suitable to most of the students.
- Most of the students get benefit from the teachings done during the PCP.

5.3.6 Study Centre

- The Distance Education Institute has no study centre of its own. However, PCP centres wherein only face to face teaching and annual examinations are held act as study centres in a very limited way.
- In the study centre of OU facilities such as study materials reference books, play back of audio and video cassettes including radio are available for the benefit of students.
- The Coordinator and Assistant coordinators of study centre in OU are part time staff and they are available on a fixed time as decided.
- The functions of study centre include sale of admission kits, organising face to face teaching on counselling and academic and administrative matters, support distance learning through the use of Audio-visual aids and submission of assignments, etc.
- Around 25 to 50 percent students make use of the study centres.
- Most of the students of OU utilize the study centres mainly for tutoring and counselling purposes followed by face to face teaching.
- Only a small proportion of students of OU utilize the facilities such as audio-video cassettes and library facilities.

- Most students suggested that the opening timing of study centres should suit the working people and its timing should be increased.
- The library facilities in the study centre should include borrowing of at least 2 to 3 books.
- One very interesting suggestion was that fees and forms be submitted at the study centre and it should act as a single window system for everything.

5.3.7 Other Support System

- Both the Distance Education Institute and Open University do not offer any pre-enrolment guidance and counselling to its students.
- Pre-enrolment guidance and counselling in being offered by the Open University, UK and Fern University, Germany on a regular basis.
- Neither Distance Education Institute nor Open Unviersity contacts the students who are either non-starter or dropouts.
- The initiative of counselling the dropout students is left to the students. When ever they approach the institute, guidance is given accordingly.
- It is found that sometimes Open University sends pre-produced letters of encouragement to its students.

5.4 CONCLUSIONS/RECOMMENDATIONS

Distance Education is a multimedia teaching-learning system which has established its academic and economic viability. This innovative system has earned credibility all over the world as an effective alternate channel for imparting education at all levels to varied clientele and target groups. This system is of special relevance to the developing countries for meeting the future educational demands of the people and for coping with the urgent needs of updating knowledge and skills of in-service persons in various professions. Unfortunately the vast potential of distance education has not been fully exploited by the Distance Education Institutes run by the Conventional Universities in our country. While the enrolment figure has gone up dramatically in these institutes, proportionately the provision of Student Support Services has not been met adequately.

On the basis of the findings of the present study, discussions with a few eminent educationists from the national Open University as well as State Open University, as also some directors and faculty members of distance education institutes, the researchers' own experience as a faculty in the Distance Education Institute of a Conventional University, and the general impressions about distance education at the national and international levels, the following recommendations are made, for the consideration of all those who are responsible for the proper development of distance education in India.

5.4.1 Recommendations on Study Materials

1. The study materials of Distance Education Institute must be subjected to thorough scrutiny and editing to ensure that they conform to self-instructional and distance education format and introduction of Course Team approach.
2. The course writers must be given training in how to write in self-instructional format.
3. The study material should be supplemented by radio talks, television programmes, audio and video cassettes.
4. The study materials should be sent to the students by registered post to those who may not collect it personally from the institute.
5. Delay in delivery of study materials must be avoided as it is bound to affect the motivation of students and bring bad name to the institute.
6. Complaints of the non-receipt of study materials should be promptly attended to by the distribution sections of the institute.
7. Arrangements must be made, to obtain feedback from the students for bringing about changes/ improvements in the lessons subsequently.
8. The institute must prepare study materials in self-instructional format in all the subjects it offers to its students and should not offer any course in which it does not have study materials.

9. IGNOU has set a good model in preparation of study materials for which Commonwealth of Learning has bestowed excellence in study material award. Therefore, the Distance Education Institute could follow the IGNOU pattern with same variations to suit local conditions/requirements.
10. However, on the basis of feedback from some students, the OU must gear up: (i) to add colour to the diagrams and charts, (ii) to give contemporary examples, (iii) to introduce latest developments instead of reprinting, and (iv) to reduce the size of the course units.
11. The Distance Education Institute should have a Material Production and Distribution Division on the pattern of IGNOU with some variations to suit local requirements.

5.4.2 Recommendations on Assignments

(1) Submission of a requisite number of assignments should be compulsory as stipulated in the UGC guidelines and the marks obtained by the students should count towards the final assessment in the ratio of 25 : 75, i.e. 75 percent being the weight for the final examinations.

(2) The evaluation of students' assignments should be carried out very carefully, pointing out the mistakes, the points left out in answers, etc. The evaluator must give constructive comments. Negative remarks should be avoided as they discourage students.

(3) The turn around time for the corrected assignments should not exceed one month.

(4) Assignment questions must be given alongwith the study materials.

5.4.3 Recommendations on PCP

(1) The Distance Education Institute must have adequate physical facilities including building for holding PCPs, counselling sessions and orientation programme for students.

(2) Adequate face-to-face contact should be provided

through organising personal contact programme to help students overcome the feeling of isolation and pursue their studies satisfactorily.

(3) PCPs should be organised for a period of 3 months each in the beginning and towards the end of the year.

(4) Teachers teaching during PCP should be oriented as they are not supposed to give formal lectures on the subject but a condensed version.

(5) PCPs should be organised in all the subjects. Subjects in which there are less number of students, intensive counselling may be suggested.

(6) Attendance at PCPs for technical/professional subjects should be compulsory.

(7) Timing and place of PCPs should be convenient to the students.

(8) Depending upon the number of students, more number of PCP centres should be opened up where the number exceeds more than 200 students.

5.4.4 Recommendations on Study Centre

(1) Each Distance Education Institute must have proper and well equipped study centres, one per 500 students.

(2) Each Study centre should have a well stocked library with multiple copies of study materials, reference books, and adequate reading room facilities and also the facility of borrowing books.

(3) The study centre should be manned by a part time coordinator who should be responsible for organising all the activities.

(4) Each study centre should act as an information centre of the Distance Education Institute, and provide the necessary information, brouchers and admission forms of various courses.

(5) As far as possible, study centres should be located in the buildings of the existing colleges. They should be easily available to the students.

5.4.5 Other Recommendations

(1) The Distance Education Institute as well as Open

University should make provision of pre-enrolment guidance and counselling for the prospective distance students in the lines of the induction programmes organised by the IGNOU immediately after the admissions are over to brief them about the University, the course and other requirements.

(2) The Distance Education Institute as well as the Open University must contact the non-starter and dropouts to bring them back to the fold of education once again.

(3) It was observed that the Distance Education Institute has accumulated surplus budget over the last so many years. This should be utilisied for improving the organisatinal set-up, and Student Support Services.

5.4.6 Recommendations on Student Support Services

Student Support Services

The four components of Student Support Services can be conceived as being in relation to each other as in Figure 5.1. They interact in complex ways. All these four need to be framed together if effective services are to be provided.

FIGURE 5.1

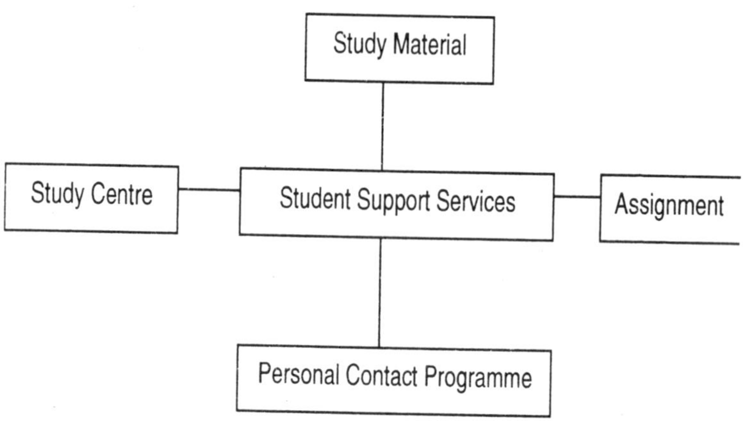

These four elements cannot be ranked in priority, nor can one element be ignored.

5.4.7 Recommendations on Functions Related to Student Support Services

At Headquarters

- Planning, execution and monitoring of Student Support Services.
- Provision of adequate and appropriate physical, financial and human resources.
- Staff development/training/orientation activities for study centre staff.
- Exploration of new strategies and diversified delivery systems.
- Coordination of activities of study centres.
- Liaison with concerned faculty and division sections at headquarters for smooth functioning of the system of support services.
- Dissemination of information and redressal of student grievances.
- Carrying out research on programme implementation and evaluation.
- Undertaking administrative activities relating to purchase and maintenance of equipment/ infrastructure, financial disbursement and management, recruitment of staff, maintenance of service records, and maintenance of library facilities.
- Undertaking public relation and promotional activities through press and broadcast media, and through seminars and workshops.

At Study Centres

- Organisation of counselling, and of audio-video and practical sessions.
- Identification of counsellors.
- Disbursal of remuneration to all part-time persons involved in SC activities.
- Management and maintenance of SC.
- Liaison with academic institutions and experts/ scholars.
- Evaluation of assignments and their dispatch to students; forwarding of grades to headquarters.

- Conduct examinations.
- Dissemination of information to students, prospective students, and the public.
- Provide grassroots feedback to headquarters.

5.4.8 Recommendations on Framework for the Development of Student Support Services

The framework for the development of a planning tool for Student Support Services is suggested here as being built around six core elements namely—

- Student Characteristics (gender, age, language, employment status, educational background special needs, etc.)
- Course demands (continuous assessment, grading, face to face element, practical, etc.)
- Geography (location of the institution, rural and urban area, density of population, cost of transport, etc.)
- Technology (technologies available to institutions and students postal, telephone, e-mail, ICT, etc.)
- Scale (volume of activity, enrolment figure numbers of courses, etc.)
- Management system (types of institutions, single/dual mode universities, etc.)

FIGURE 5.2

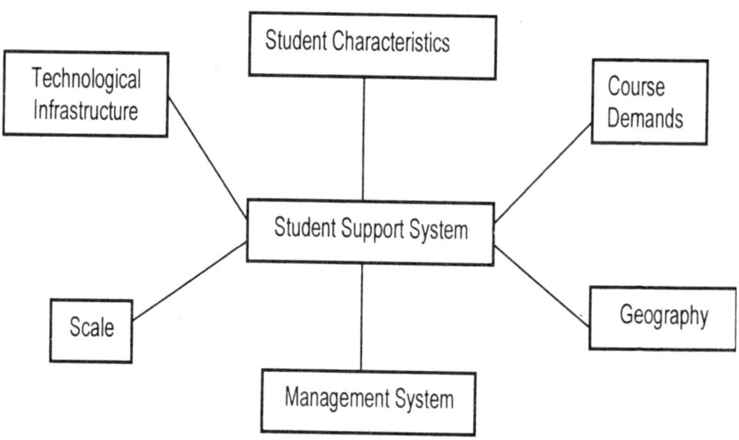

The six elements of Student Support Services can be conceived as being in relation to teach other as in Figure 5.2. The six elements of the basic framework for planning student support interact in complex ways. They cannot be ranked in priority, nor can one element be ignored. Thus while course demands may be the first to be conceived by those planning education, these will need to be framed along with the other five dimensions if effective services are to be provided.

5.4.9 Recommendation on Design for Distance Education Institute

Student Support Services are a cluster of facilities and activities that should be started to make the learning process easier and more interesting for the student. In a Distance Education, they serve as the interface between the institution and the learner. The organisation and functioning of Student Support Services is related to the activities/products of different sub-systems of Distance Education. Therefore, it is suggested that the Distance Education Institute should have the design as given in Figure 5.3.

FIGURE 5.3

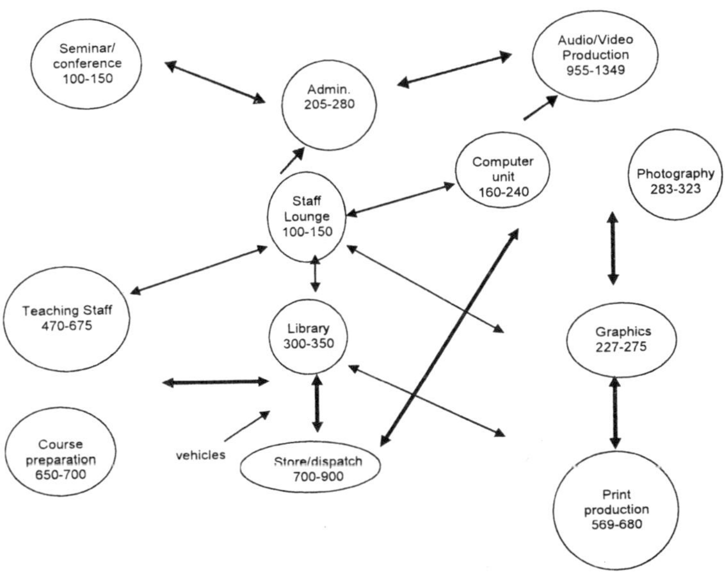

5.5 SUGGESTIONS FOR FURTHER RESEARCH

No research is the last word in a particular field of study nor can it give final verdict about the phenomenon and hence scope for further work is always there. It is therefore, hoped that the present piece of research would stimulate some researchers to take up researches on the issues pertaining to various dimensions of distance education, e.g. instructional systems in distance education, evaluation system of distance education characteristics and performance of distance learners, etc. The following suggestions for further research are suggested:

(1) A study of the existing audio-visual facilities and its impact on studies may be taken up.
(2) A study relating to the processes of continuous evaluation as exists in the distance education system may be taken up.
(3) A comparative study of Student Support Services among different State Open Universities may result in useful data.
(4) A detailed study on students' dropout from the distance education system may be taken up.
(5) Attitudinal study of distance learners towards various Student Support Services.
(6) A feedback study on utilization of various facilities and services at the study centres may be taken up.
(7) An investigation into the problems of academic counsellors with regard to assessment response sheets and comments on them could be taken out.
(8) A detailed study into the organization and participation in PCP may be conducted.

Bibliography

Anand, S. (1979), *"University without Walls"* : The Indian Perspective in Correspondence Education, Vikas, New Delhi.

Balasubramaniam, S. (1986), "The Status of correspondence courses in India", *University News*, Vol. 24, No. 12, pp. 13-15, AIU, New Delhi.

Bartels, J. (1982), "Absolvenen", Hagen, Fernuniversitat, ZFE.

Beardsley (1975), "The Free University of Iran" in Mackenzie, N., *et. al.* (ed.) *Open Learning*, Paris, Unesco Press.

Best, J.W. *et. al.* (1978), "Research in Education", Prentice Hall of India, New Delhi.

Biswal B.N. (1979), *"A Study of Correspondence Education in Indian Universities"*, Ph.D. Thesis, M.S. University, Baroda.

Brindley, J. (1995), "Learners and Learner Services : The Key to the Future in Open and Distance Learning", in Roberts, J.M and Keough, E.R (Eds.) *Why the Information Highway? Lessons for Open and Distance Learning*, Trifolium, Toronto.

Buch, M.B. (1991) (ed.), *"Fourth Survey of Research in Education"*, NCERT, New Delhi.

Chandhok, S. (1995), "Role of Libraries in Distance Teaching Universities : A Study of Students' Problems", in Panda, S.K. *et. al.* (eds.), *Indian Distance Education : Contemporary Research*, New Delhi.

Childs, G.B. (1960), *"An Annotated Bibliography of Correspondence Study, 1897-1960"*, National University Extension Association, New York.

Cookson, Peter S. (1989), "Research on Learners and Learning in Distance Education : A Review", *American Journal of Distance Education*, Vol. 3, No. 2, pp. 22-34.

Datt, R. (1976), *"Correspondence Courses in India"*, Winged Words, University of Delhi, New Delhi.

———, (1984), "Planning and Development of Distance Education", *Journal of Higher Education*, Vol. 9, No. 3, pp. 305-14.

Denscombe, M. (1999), *"The Good Research Guide for Small Scale Social Research Projects"*, Viva, New Delhi.

Deshpande, P.M. (1994), "Quality Assurance in Higher Education", *The COL/DEC Report*, DEC, IGNOU, New Delhi.

Devi, U. (1994), "Are Contact Sessions Necessary in Distance Education"? *Indian Journal of Open Learning*, Vol. 3, No. 1, pp. 16-21.

Dewal, O.S. (1982), *"Profile of Registration: An Enquiry into Variables Related to Students of Correspondence Institutes at the Secondary Level"*, Open School, CBSE, New Delhi.

Dikshit, H.P. (2002), "Addressing Access and Equity through Open and Flexibe Learning : Initiatives and Challenges", XV *Annual Conference of the Asian Association of Open Universities*. Address by IGNOU Vice-Chancellor.

Dillman, D.A. (1987), "Response to Mail Surveys : what we know, what we don't know, and what we need to find out?" Paper read at ZUMA—Konferenz, Manheim, April 17-30.

Escotet, M. (1980) "Adverse factors in the development of an Open University in Latin America", *Programme Learning and Educational Technology*, Vol. 17, No. 4, pp. 262-70.

European Association of Distance Teaching Universities (1994), *"European Open University Network—An Introduction"*, EADTU, Netherland.

European Association of Distance Teaching Universities (1994), *"EADTU—News"*, Heerlen, Vol. 17, July

European Association of Distance Teaching Universities (1994), "EADTU—An Introduction", EADTU, Netherland.

European Association of Distance Teaching Universities (1993/1994), *"Mini Directory"*, EADTU, Netherland.

Friedman, Z. (1981), "Systems for student administration", in A. Kaye and G. Rumble (Eds.), *Distance Teaching for Higher and Adult Education*, Croomhelm, London.

Gough, E. (1984), "Towards a Philosophy of Distance Education", in Smith, K. (ed.) *Diversity down under in Distance Education*. Toowoomba : Darling Downs Insitute.

Guri, S. (1993), "Quality Assurance Procedures in Developing Academic Courses : A comparative Study of Five Distance Teaching University", in A. Tait (ed.) *Quality Assurance in Open and Distance Learning: European and International Perspectives*, Conference papers, Open University, Cambridge, London.

Harichandan, D. (1990), *"Working of the Study Centres : A comparative study of IGNOU and YCMOU"*, Project Report of Post MA Diploma in Adult and Continuing Education, SNDTW University, Mumbai.

———, (1993), "Learners Perspective of Distance Education : Implications for Strengthening Student Support Services". Journal of Educational Planning and Administration, Vol. VII, No 4, pp. 475-85.

———, (1993), "Working of the Study Centres : A comparative study of two Open Universities". *Media and Technology for Human Resource Development*, Vol. 5, No. 4, pp. 285-92.

———, (2004), "A Study of Student Support Services in Distance Education Institute of Conventional University and Open University". Ph.D. Thesis, YCMOU, Nashik.

Holmberg, B. (1960), *"On the method of Teaching by Correspondence"*, Lunds Universities, N.F. Lund.

Holmberg, B. (1985), *"Status and Trends of Distance Education"*. Lector Publishing, Lund.

Holmberg, B. (1987), "The Development of Distance Education Research", *American Journal of Distance Education*, Vol. 1, No. 3, pp. 16-23.

Holmberg, B. (1989), *"Theory and Practice of Distance Education"*, Routledge and Kegan Paul, London.

Holmberg, B. (1990), *"Perspectives of Research on Distance Education"*, 2nd Edition , Zentrales Institute for Fernstudien for Schung (ZIFF), Hagen.

Institute of Distance Education (1997), *"Institute of Distance Education Silver Jubliee Year (1996-97) Souvenir"*, University of Mumbai, Mumbai.

Institute of Distance Education (2002), *"IDE Prospectus for B.A."*, University of Mumbai, Mumbai.

IGNOU (1996), *"A Proposal on Channels of Learning and Delivery in Open University System,* IGNOU, New Delhi.

IGNOU (2000), *"Indira Gandhi National Open University : A Profile—(2000)"*, IGNOU, New Delhi.

IGNOU 2002, *"XV Annual Conference of the AAOU Conference Souvenir"*, February 21-23, 2002, New Delhi.

Khan, I. (1982), *"Suitability of Teaching English through Correspondence Courses as Offered by some Indian Universities at the first degree level"*, Ph.D. Thesis, Utkal University, Bhubaneswar.

Koul, B.N. and Ramanujam, P.R. (1989) , *"IGNOU Hand Book 1– Distance Education"*, Division of Distance Education, IGNOU, New Delhi.

Kumar, K. *et. al.* (1986), *"Motivation of B.Ed. Correspondence Students"*, NCERT, New Delhi.

Kumar, J.P. and Rao, D.B. (1998), *"Effectiveness of Distance Education System"*, Discovery, New Delhi.

Kumar, J.P., Rao, D.B. and Rao, G.S. (2000), *"Open University : Student Support Services"*, Discovery, New Delhi.

Mani, G. (1989), "Attitudes of External Faculty towards Distance Education", Paper presented at ICDE Conference.

Marland, P. (1989), "An Apporach to Research on Distance Learning", *British Journal of Education Technology,* Vol. 20, No. 3, pp. 173-82

Mills, R. and Tait, A. (Eds.) (1997), *"Supporting the Learner in Open and Distance Learning"*, Pitman, London.

Minnis, John R. (1985), "Ethnography, Case Study, Grounded Theory and Distance Education Research", *Distance Education : An International Journal,* Vol. VI, No. 2, pp. 189-98.

Moore, Michael G. (1985), "Some Observation on Current Research in Distance Education", *Epistolodidaktika,* Vol. 1, pp. 32-62.

Morgan, A. (1984), "A Report on Qualitative Methodologies in Research in Distance Education", *Distance Education: An International Journal*, Vol. V, No. 2, pp. 252-67.

Mukhopadhyay, M (1990), "A mixed Fare", *University News*, Vol. 28, November.

Nagaraju, C.S. (1982), *"Evaluation of Radio Correspondences-cum-Contact Inservice Teacher Training Programme in Kerala"*, Institute for Social and Economic Change, Bangalore.

Nonyongo, E. and Ngengebule, A. (1998), *"Learner Support Services : Case Studies of DEASA Member Institutions*, UNISA, Pretoria.

Panda, S.K. (1991), "Distance Educational Research in India : Stock-taking, Concerns and Prospects," *Distance Education. An International Journal*, Vol. 3, No. 2, pp. 309-26.

Paul, R. (1990), *"Open Learning and Open Management : Leadership and integrity in D.E."*, Kogan Page, London.

Perry, Walter (1976), *"Open University : A Personal Account by the First Vice-Chancellor"*, The Open University Press, Milton Keynes.

Rathore, H.C.S. (1993), *"Management of Distance Education in India"*, Ashish, New Delhi.

Robinson, B. (1981) , "Support for Student Learning", in Kaye, A. and Rumble, G. (Eds.), *Distance Teaching for Higher and Adult Education*, Croom Helon, London.

Rumble, G. (1992), *"The Management of Distance Learning Systems"*, UNESCO/International Institute for Educational Planning, Paris.

Rumble, G. (1997), *"The Costs and Economics of Open and Distance Education"*, Kogan Page, London.

Sahoo, P.K. (1985), "A study of Correspondence Education in an Indian University", Ph.D. Thesis, M.S. University, Baroda.

Sahoo, P.K. (1991), "Research in Distance Education at University level in India," *Perspectives in Education*, Vol. 7, No. 2, pp. 71-88.

SAIDE (2000), *"Learner Support in Distance Learning, A South African Programme Perspective : A study for the South African Institute for Distance Education"*, SAIDE, Johannesburg.

Sashi (1972), *"A Comparative Study of Achievement of Students Passing through Correspondence Courses and Regular Courses"*, M.A. Dissertation, Kurukshetra University, Kurukshetra.

Sewart, D. (1978), "Continuity of concern for students studying at a Distance", *ZIFF Papiere,* 18, Hagen : Fernuniversitat.

Sewart, D. (1993), "Student Support Systems in D.E.", *Open Learning,* Vol. 8, No. 3, pp. 3-12.

Singh, H.N. and Panda, S.K. (1980), "The Philosophy of Correspondence Education", *Education Quarterly,* Vol. 32, No. 4, October, pp. 27-29.

Singh, J. (1983), *"A Study of the Correspondence Eduation Programme of the Board of Secondary Education, Ajmer, Rajasthan"*, Centre for Educational Technology, February, 1980 page NCERT, New Delhi.

Srinivasacharyula, G. and Rammaiah, P. (1992), "Face to face support services at BR Amedker Open University : Student response, *Media and Technology for Human Resource Development,* Vol. 5, No. 1, pp. 41-47.

Sweet, R. (1993), *"Student Support Services : Towards more Respective Systems,* Perspectives on D.E., Commonwealth of Learning, Vancouver.

Tait, A. (2000), "Planning Student Support for Open and Distance Learning" *Open Learning,* Vol. 15, No. 3, pp. 287-99.

UGC (1985), *"Guidelines for Introduction of Correspondence Courses"*, Mimeographed.

UKOU (1994), *"Report of the Vice-Chancellor,* UKOU, Milton Keynes, UK.

University of Mumbai (2000), *"University of Mumbai : A Profile 2000"*, Mumbai.

Vijaya Lakshmi, B. and Raju, N. (1993), "The Library System in an Open University : An Evaluation of Library Facilities, Resources and Services", *Kakatiya Journal of Distance Education,* Vol. 2, No. 2, pp. 63-70.

Williams, J. and Williams, M. (1987), "Student Operated Network for Distance Learners", *ICDI Bulletin,* Vol. 13, January, pp. 51-64.

Index